Narcissistic Abuse:

The Complete Guide to Recovering From Narcissistic Abuse — Discover How to Identify Narcissism in Ourselves and Others to Avoid Toxic Relationships

Sharon Heal

© **Copyright 2019 - All rights reserved.**

The content contained within this book may not be reproduced, duplicated or transmitted without direct written permission from the author or the publisher.

Under no circumstances will any blame or legal responsibility be held against the publisher, or author, for any damages, reparation, or monetary loss due to the information contained within this book. Either directly or indirectly.

Legal Notice:

This book is copyright protected. This book is only for personal use. You cannot amend, distribute, sell, use, quote or paraphrase any part, or the content within this book, without the consent of the author or publisher.

Disclaimer Notice:

Please note the information contained within this document is for educational and entertainment purposes only. All effort has been executed to present accurate, up to date, and reliable, complete information. No warranties of any kind are declared or implied. Readers acknowledge that the author is not engaging in the rendering of legal, financial, medical or professional advice. The content within this book has been derived from various sources. Please consult a licensed professional before attempting any techniques outlined in this book.

By reading this document, the reader agrees that under no circumstances is the author responsible for any losses, direct or indirect, which are incurred as a result of the use of information contained within this document, including, but not limited to, — errors, omissions, or inaccuracies

Table of Contents

Introduction
Chapter 1: What Is Narcissistic Abuse?

Types of Abuse
Recognizing Abusive Behaviors

Harmful Words
Manipulative Actions
Taking Advantage of You
Ignoring Boundaries
Isolating
Undermining
Control
Dishonesty
The Narcissistic Abuser

Chapter 2: What Narcissists Do

The Cycle of Abuse
The Five Stages of Abuse
Methods of Control

Superficial Charm
Love Bombing
Nagging
Ignoring
Punishment
Guilt Tripping
Emotional Blackmail Tactics
Isolation Tactics
Mind Games
Gaslighting
Blaming the Victim

The Big Picture

Chapter 3: Why Are Some People Narcissistic?

Healthy Ego
Narcissistic Parenting

Effects on the Child
Parenting Styles

Narcissistic Entitlement
Other Factors
Problems Associated with Narcissism

Chapter 4: How Narcissists Think

Types of Narcissists

The Normal Narcissist
The Unprincipled Narcissist
The Amorous Narcissist
The Elitist Narcissist
The Compensatory Narcissist
The Hedonistic Narcissist
The Fanatic Narcissist
The Spiritual Narcissist
The Malignant Narcissist

Grandiose or Vulnerable?
How to Know If You're a Narcissist

Chapter 5: Who Do Narcissists Target?

The Symptoms of Codependency
How Does Codependency Develop?
The Appeal of the Narcissist
Narcissistic Friends and Family Members
Enabling
How Do Narcissists Recognize Codependent People?

Chapter 6: Dealing with a Narcissist

Effective Responses
Clarify Your Boundaries
Assert Yourself
Projection

Dealing with Narcissistic Parents

Ineffective Responses
Don't Placate
Don't Argue
Don't Defend
Don't Criticize
Don't Beg
Don't Blame Yourself
Don't Bluff
Don't Deny It
Don't Avoid It
Don't Look for Sympathy or Understanding

Dealing with Physical Abuse

Chapter 7: Next Steps

Boundary Checking
Rebuilding Your Self-Esteem
Should I Stay, or Should I Go?
Leaving an Abusive Relationship
Toxic Family Relationships

Chapter 8: Long-Term Effects of Narcissistic Abuse

Effects of Abuse
Narcissist Victim Syndrome
Effects on the Brain
Post-Traumatic Stress Disorder
Self-Isolation After Narcissistic Abuse

Chapter 9: Recovering from Narcissistic Abuse

Waking Up
Breaking Contact
Understanding What Happened
Healing
Starting Over

Chapter 10: 7 Tips to Avoid Toxic Relationships

Don't Rush
Stay on Guard
Don't Make Yourself Responsible for Other People
Don't Make Other People Responsible for You
Watch Out for Red Flags
Be Wary of Your Blind Spots
Listen Up

Conclusion

Introduction

Congratulations on downloading *Narcissistic Abuse: The Complete Guide to Healing after Narcissistic Abuse,* and thank you for doing so! Narcissistic Personality Disorder is surprisingly common, affecting up to 6% of the population. People with this disorder can seem charming and self-confident, but their excessive need for admiration from others masks deeper insecurity and self-loathing that drives them to manipulate and abuse the people who care about them.

The following chapters will discuss the symptoms of narcissistic abuse, the strategies that narcissistic abusers use to manipulate their victims, the traumatic childhood experiences that cause this disorder, and the distorted thinking patterns typical of the narcissist.

This book will also teach you about codependency, as well as why narcissists so often target codependent people. In addition, this book will teach you effective tips and strategies for dealing with narcissists, how to rebuild your self-esteem after narcissistic abuse, how to get out of an abusive relationship, how to deal with Narcissistic

Victim Syndrome and its long-term effects, how to heal the wounds from an abusive relationship, and how to avoid toxic relationships in the future.

Narcissistic abuse can cause tremendous damage, but the information in *Narcissistic Abuse: The Complete Guide* can help you make sense of what happened and get started on the path to long-term healing and personal freedom.

There are plenty of books on this subject on the market—thanks again for choosing this one! Every effort was made to ensure it is full of as much useful information as possible. Please enjoy!

Chapter 1: What Is Narcissistic Abuse?

In Greek mythology, Narcissus was the most handsome man who ever lived. Everyone who saw the young hunter fell in love with him, but Narcissus was incapable of loving anyone. One day, on a hunting trip, a nymph named Echo confessed her love to him. He rejected her so cruelly that she shriveled up and disappeared, leaving only her voice behind. Later, Narcissus happened to see his own reflection in a pool of water and was so captivated by his own beauty that he stared into the pool until he wasted away.

All of us, at some point, have known a narcissist. A narcissist is a person with a distorted and ultimately false self-image, just like the reflection that Narcissus saw in the pond. The self-image of the narcissist is overblown—smarter, more competent, and more beautiful than any normal person. Despite what seems to be egotistical self-admiration, the narcissist desperately needs approval and validation from other people. In the end, he doesn't really believe his own self-image. The narcissist feels an uncontrollable compulsion to be loved and praised and will seek out relationships for the sole purpose of getting this need met by any means necessary.

Just like the good-looking but heartless young man in the Greek myth, the narcissist is unbelievably charming but basically empty—in love with his own reflection. Like the nymph in the story, anyone unfortunate enough to love such a person risks fading away into a mere echo.

Unlike Narcissus, real narcissists don't just reject their victims. All too often, the narcissist will go out of his way to make you emotionally dependent on him before systematically destroying your sense of self-esteem to ensure that you never abandon him. The narcissist's abusive behavior can eventually leave you too confused and filled with doubt to consider leaving the relationship. In effect, the narcissist reduces you to an echo of his own thoughts and needs—all the while remaining focused on his own image.

Narcissistic abuse is profoundly damaging, with negative effects that can last for years. The children of narcissistic parents sometimes repeat the destructive pattern, either as victims or as abusers. Narcissists almost always blame others for their own actions, so it's uncommon for a narcissist to seek professional help.

Not all abusers are narcissistic, but abusive behaviors have certain characteristics in common regardless of the abuser's motivation. The key to protecting yourself from narcissistic abuse is to recognize what constitutes abusive behavior.

Types of Abuse

There are many different types of abusive behavior, but most abuse fits into one of four major categories.

Physical abuse is any form of physical violence or restraint. This includes not only obvious behaviors like punching, kicking, or shoving—but it's also comprised of less obvious behaviors such as holding you in place to prevent you from leaving or punching a hole in the wall to frighten and intimidate you.

Sexual abuse is any violation of your sexual boundaries or autonomy, including the use of pressure and manipulation to get you to consent to sexual contact.

Neglect is the failure to provide care when it is the person's responsibility to do so. For instance, parents who don't provide adequate food and clothing or who don't set healthy rules and boundaries to keep the child safe may be neglecting the child. Narcissistic parents often neglect their children, as they see their children primarily as sources of the love and admiration that they need rather than as individual human beings who need to be cared for and protected.

Emotional abuse refers to words and behaviors that harm the victim's psychological well-being, such as verbal abuse and manipulative behavior. Physical and sexual abuse is often combined with emotional abuse, but emotional abuse can also occur on its own. Emotional abuse is subtler and harder to define than physical or sexual abuse. If someone hits you or touches you without your consent, then they are obviously abusive to you—but it's much harder to say when words and other behaviors cross the line. Despite being subtler, emotional abuse can be just as harmful as other forms of abuse—or even more so.

Recognizing Abusive Behaviors

Abuse can sometimes be hard to recognize because a lot of abusive behaviors occur on a spectrum with less extreme behaviors that are not necessarily harmful or malicious enough to be considered abusive. Almost everyone has said or done something passive-aggressive or manipulative when frustrated. Almost everyone has said something insulting or overly critical when angry. These behaviors are not ideal, but they aren't always an example of abuse.

Thus, how do you know when someone is abusing you? You have to make a judgment call based on the big picture of your relationship with the person, and how pervasive and destructive the behaviors are. One or two incidents in isolation might not constitute abuse, but if you suspect something about the relationship is toxic, you should look for the warning signs. Potentially abusive behaviors include harmful words, manipulative actions, taking advantage of you, ignoring your boundaries, isolating you from your support networks, undermining your goals and dreams, trying to control you, and dishonest behavior.

Harmful Words

People can use words to hurt each other in dozens of different ways, from excessive criticism to insulting comments. Verbal abuse can look like anything from over-the-top rage to a coldly calm expression of disdain and contempt.

An abuser may say things to put you down, accuse you of doing things you didn't do, blame you for things that aren't really your fault, compare you to other people in a demeaning way, interrupt you whenever you try to express yourself, or give you commands like a drill sergeant. Shaming is one of the most common forms of abusive behavior from a narcissistic parent.

Sometimes, verbal abuse can be subtler than this, like disagreeing with everything you say or making so many demands that you constantly feel inadequate. Other times verbal abuse isn't subtle at all and may even include threats or openly bullying behaviors. Verbal abuse can also include putting you down in front of other people, spreading unflattering stories about you, or encouraging other people to make fun of you or exclude you in some way.

There are so many different types of verbal abuse that it would be impossible to list them all, but they all have one thing in common. The abuser gains more power in the relationship through harmful words, and the abused person feels smaller and smaller for as long as the abuse continues.

How can you tell whether something constitutes abuse or not? The important point to consider here is how malicious the behavior seems. For instance, there's a big difference between an occasional sarcastic comment and a pattern of constant, demeaning sarcasm. How do you usually feel when you talk to this person? If your conversations often leave you feeling worse about yourself, you may be a victim of verbal abuse. If the person seems to be putting you down to feel better about themselves, this could be part of a pattern of narcissistic abuse. Whether the person abusing you is a narcissist or not, verbal abuse can cause tremendous damage to your self-esteem and well-being.

Manipulative Actions

Manipulative behavior can be hard to recognize because manipulation is indirect. For example, a manipulative person might offer to help you with a problem but then try to get you to feel guilty or excessively obligated to them for accepting their help. Alternatively, they might use guilt or shame to get you to do something for them.

They may seem kind and warm until you don't do what they want you to do, at which point they become cold and distant. They may withhold attention or affection so that you will pursue them, constantly forcing you to guess what they really want from you. They might use gossip and jealousy to play two friends or two siblings or two love interests against each other, a divide and conquer strategy known as "triangulation." As with verbal abuse, manipulation takes many forms.

The person being manipulated often feels like the bad guy in the situation, because that's exactly how the abuser wants them to feel. So, how can you recognize when you're being manipulated? Manipulation causes "FOG," a combination of three potent emotions—fear, obligation, and guilt. Fear that something bad will happen if you don't do what the other person wants, a sense that you owe them something for some reason, and the feeling that you will be a bad person if you don't go along with it. The result of FOG is that you doubt your own judgment, even though your instincts are telling you that something is wrong with the situation.

One of the most insidious types of manipulation is known as "gaslighting," in which the abuser manipulates you into distrusting your own memories and second-guessing your own ability to tell reality from illusion.

Taking Advantage of You

An abuser may take advantage of you financially by spending shared money without your consent, taking money out of your bank account, selling things that belong to you, or running up debts in your name. Financial abuse allows the abuser to profit by using your financial resources as their own, but it also tends to leave you impoverished and financially dependent on the abuser for your own survival.

The same dynamic can occur in any relationship where the other person has total control over the household finances, even if they aren't actually dipping into your bank account or writing checks with your name on them. Without financial independence, you're a lot less likely to leave the relationship—and the abuser knows that.

Financial abuse can also be combined with other forms of abuse, such as emotional blackmail. For example, most people are happy to help family or friends in need if the situation comes up. An abusive person will take advantage of the kindness of a friend or relative by guilt-tripping them into helping again and again whether they really need it or not. How can you tell the difference? By looking out for FOG. If you feel a combination of fear, obligation, and guilt about the request, then you should ask yourself if you are being manipulated.

Ignoring Boundaries

Manipulators and abusers will ignore your boundaries and destroy your sense of independence because they don't respect your right to establish boundaries in the first place. For an abusive narcissist, the other person in the relationship is only there to fulfill their needs, and they feel justified in doing whatever it takes to keep the person attached to them and dependent on them.

For example, a narcissistic parent might read a child's diary, or a narcissistic boyfriend might read his girlfriend's text messages. An abuser might go through your things without asking permission or walk in on you without knocking when you have the door closed. In general, one of the warning signs of an abusive relationship is when you try to set boundaries, and they are repeatedly ignored.

An abuser might ignore a request for more space or refuse to accept a break-up or a rejection. It can be dangerous to think of this as a simple failure of communication. Any time a person ignores your boundaries, you should consider this a serious warning sign.

Isolating

Most people have a support network of family and friends—the people we confide in and whose opinions we trust, the people we would call if we needed help. To an abuser, all these people are a potential threat. Your old college roommate might tell you that your new boyfriend sounds a little controlling. Your brother might let you crash on his couch for a while if you suddenly decide to move out. Your friends might say supportive and encouraging things that contradict the constant criticism you're being subjected to.

To prevent any of these things from happening, an abuser will systematically undermine your other relationships to leave you as isolated and dependent as possible. Behaviors intended to isolate you can take many forms, such as expecting you to constantly account for your whereabouts or suddenly "getting sick" and needing support from you when you were planning to spend time with friends. It can even involve deliberate character assassination, such as telling friends or family members lies about you.

If someone in your life is acting as a gatekeeper, making it hard for people to see you or talk to you, this may be a sign that they are trying to isolate you from your usual support networks.

Undermining

An abuser may sabotage and undermine you in various ways to keep you from achieving an independent sense of success and happiness. For example, they may "forget" to pass on an important message, or they may say embarrassing things to humiliate you in front of your friends or coworkers. It can be hard to recognize sabotaging behavior because the abuser can pretend it was all just an innocent mistake or a misunderstanding.

If you start to suspect an important person in your life of intentionally sabotaging you, step back and look at the big picture. Our loved ones are supposed to support us and help us achieve our goals and dreams. If someone you care about has a consistent pattern of getting in your way rather than helping you out, it might be sabotage.

Another form of sabotage is to compare you unkindly to other people. The abuser's goal is to undermine your self-confidence and chip away at your self-respect. The topic of comparison may probably be your looks or your cooking or how much money you make, but the message is always the same—that you don't measure up.

Why would anyone want you to feel worse about yourself? Remember, the narcissistic abuser needs an endless supply of love and praise and doesn't really believe you'll stick around of your own free will. By tearing you down, the narcissist can make you completely dependent. If someone is telling you that you are stupid or useless, that other people don't like you, or that you couldn't possibly live without them, ask yourself why they would want you to think that.

Control

In a healthy relationship, both parties have an equal level of power. Shared decisions such as whether to buy a new home or where to go on vacation are made through discussion and compromise. Both partners have the right and ability to make individual decisions, too, such as whether to spend time with friends or spend small amounts of money.

In an abusive relationship, one partner has all the power, and the other partner is effectively under their control. Major decisions are all made by the dominant partner, who also seeks to micromanage every little detail of the other person's life.

An abuser may limit the time you spend with your friends or expect you to account for every penny you spend. They may want to know where you are and what you are doing at all times. They may expect you to clear everything you do with them ahead of time and accuse you of dishonesty or infidelity if you do not.

Sometimes, the abuser establishes control through outright dominance and bullying. Sometimes, control established through subtler and indirect forms of manipulation such as sabotage and undermining. Either way, if you start to feel like you can no longer make your own decisions and have no equality in the relationship, this is a warning sign that you may be under the control of an abuser.

Dishonesty

Abusers and narcissists often accuse their partners of being unfaithful or dishonest but feel no obligation to be faithful or honest themselves. The narcissist typically sees himself as being superior to others and may, therefore, feel that the rules don't apply to him.

In addition, the narcissist is constantly looking for a new source of praise and admiration, and no one is more likely to supply this than a new person who doesn't know what the narcissist is truly like. For this reason, narcissists typically can't sustain a committed relationship for very long before they start looking around for a new source of the admiration they crave.

Projection is one of the defining characteristics of the narcissistic abuser, meaning that they will project their own negative feelings and behaviors onto other people. The narcissist tells you that you are worthless because he secretly feels worthless and accuses you of being dishonest and unfaithful because he is dishonest and unfaithful.

The Narcissistic Abuser

Narcissistic abuse can include any or all of these abusive behaviors. So, what makes any particular abusive behavior narcissistic?

It all comes down to the abuser's motivation. Not all abusers are narcissists. For instance, a sociopathic abuser is not motivated by the need for admiration or praise, but only by the desire to get whatever he wants out of the situation without regard for others. A sadistic abuser gets pleasure or amusement from causing suffering. Some abusers are motivated by a pathological need to control every aspect of life in an attempt to manage their own intense feelings of anxiety and fear. Some are mentally ill and unaware of how their actions impact the people around them.

Whatever the reason for the abuse, the abuser is always responsible for their own actions. The victim is never at fault for the abuse. To the victim of abuse, it may not matter much whether the abuser is motivated by narcissism or sociopathy or something else. Getting free of the abuse is what really matters.

However, recognizing patterns can sometimes be a crucial step in learning how to break out of them for good. If you've been the victim of narcissistic abuse, understanding what happened and how it happened can help you move on. It may help you avoid a similar situation in the future, or it may help you avoid repeating the pattern by abusing others.

The narcissistic abuser is motivated by a deep sense of shame and self-loathing, leading them to create a mask or an imaginary version of the self that is far superior to other people. Because the narcissist secretly knows that this imaginary self isn't real at all, they need constant reassurance in the form of love and admiration from others to sustain the illusion. The narcissist abuses others to prop up this false self, using tactics you can learn to recognize.

Chapter 2: What Narcissists Do

The Cycle of Abuse

The key to understanding narcissistic abuse is to understand what the narcissist is looking for in a relationship. Narcissists are always looking for someone to admire them, someone to reinforce the ideal self they've created. This feeling of being admired and praised is called "narcissistic supply," and everything the narcissist does is done for the purpose of either maintaining one source of narcissistic supply or cultivating a new source.

In parent-to-child narcissistic relationships, the narcissistic parent treats the child as a permanent source of narcissistic supply and does everything possible to prevent the child from ever becoming an independent person through guilt-tripping, belittling, and other abusive behaviors.

In adult-to-adult narcissistic relationships, the narcissist comes on strong in the early stages with an idealized and ultimately imaginary version of his real personality. The ideal self isn't real, so the narcissist won't be able to keep up the façade. The true self slips out, and the narcissist does something abusive and damaging. When the mask is restored, the victim is once again shown the idealized self. This emotional roller coaster can result in something called "trauma bonding," where the victim actually gets emotionally closer to the abuser as a result of the abuse. Even though the victim may want to believe that the idealized version of the narcissist is real, and the abusive behavior is the exception, the truth is the exact opposite.

In the end, the narcissist will seek out a new source of narcissistic supply, discarding the old relationship as if it never meant anything. In some cases, the narcissist will hover in the background rather than completely disappearing. By going away and then coming back, the narcissist can keep the victim from ever moving on and ensure his own access to the narcissistic supply.

The Five Stages of Abuse

The cycle of abuse can be divided into five stages, marked by different types of abusive behavior—some of which will not appear abusive at first. The first stage is gaining trust, in which the abuser idealizes the victim and acts loving, kind, and sweet. In cases of narcissistic abuse, this is when the narcissist will present only the false or idealized self.

The second stage is over-involvement, in which the abuser works his way into every little detail of the victim's life. Healthy boundaries are slowly eroded until the victim can no longer tell what a boundary violation is and what is not.

The third stage is rulemaking, in which the abuser sets the terms of the relationship through jealous and controlling behavior. This is presented by the abuser as an expression of their love for the victim, but the level of jealousy and micromanaging extends far beyond normal relationship insecurity.

The fourth stage deals with control, in which the abuser gains power over the victim through all kinds of abuse and manipulation. Most of the obviously abusive behaviors don't occur until this stage when the victim already has a diminished ability to recognize and respond to what is happening.

The fifth stage is trauma bonding, where the abuser once again presents the ideal self for a time to draw the victim closer again.

Methods of Control

Once you understand that the abuser's manipulative and controlling behaviors are part of a pattern, it should be easier to recognize specific abusive behaviors for what they are. The narcissistic abuser's methods of control include:

- Superficial charm
- Love bombing
- Nagging
- Ignoring
- Punishment
- Guilt Tripping
- Emotional Blackmail
- Isolation
- Mind Games
- Gaslighting
- Blaming the Victim

Superficial Charm

"Superficial charm" is the narcissist's version of courtship behavior. The narcissist is slick and likable, but there is nothing behind it because the charming behavior is only an expression of the false self the narcissist has created. Narcissistic parents may use superficial charm when interacting with anyone outside the household, such as teachers or social workers. In a dating relationship, the narcissist uses superficial charm to gain the victim's trust.

Narcissists in the early stages of a relationship may appear to be unusually romantic, attentive, and complimentary. They may seem to idealize you or to have a lot in common with you—perhaps too much to be completely believable. One tactic of psychological control is "ingratiation," in which the abuser gains your trust by deliberately mirroring your likes and dislikes.

In reality, these behaviors are all part of the act. It isn't easy to tell the difference between superficial charm and genuine good-will, but if your instincts are telling you that something is off, then you should slow down and pay close attention to other red flags such as "love bombing."

Love Bombing

The term "love bombing" originally referred to as a recruitment tactic used by some cult groups. Potential members of the cult would be drawn in through intense displays of positive attention and affection combined with strong pressure to join the group. Later on, mental health counselors started to use the term to describe a similar tactic often used by narcissistic abusers.

To a lonely person looking for love and affection, a sudden and over-the-top display of love can be like a drug. It feels so good that you just want more. The narcissist knows this and uses the "love bomb" to draw the victim in. The intense positive attention is combined with pressure to commit quickly, escalating the relationship to a higher level much faster than most people would usually be comfortable with.

The combination of affection and pressure creates a sense of anxiety, as the victim doesn't want to miss out on the chance at "true love" by resisting the narcissist's wishes. The pressure to commit is also a test, in which the narcissist is trying to find out whether the target will set a firm boundary or not. When the victim gives in to the pressure and agrees to a commitment, the narcissist is already in the second stage of abuse—the stage of over-involvement.

Of course, it can be hard to tell whether someone is love bombing you or genuinely falling in love with you. The main difference is consistency. Love bombing is shallow and is always followed by devaluation. From being idealized, you become the object of contempt and derision. Real love isn't like that, but the only certain way to tell the difference between the two is to wait and see. That's why it's so important not to get carried away and escalate the relationship too quickly—especially if you're feeling pressured.

Nagging

Superficial charm and love bombing are both types of positive reinforcement, in which you are rewarded with positive attention for doing what the abuser wants you to do. Nagging is a type of negative reinforcement in which you are pressured to do what the abuser wants you to do.

Nagging isn't always abusive. Parents nag children to clean up their rooms, and children nag parents for candy or screen time. As annoying as that can be, it doesn't constitute abuse. Abusive nagging happens when you try to set a healthy boundary, and the abuser wears your boundary down with repeated requests. Like many other kinds of subtle manipulation, nagging always has plausible deniability. If you call out the narcissist for pushing your boundaries, she can always claim that she was "only asking" and accuse you of being oversensitive.

In a healthy relationship, some decisions are shared equally between both parties, and some decisions are yours alone. You may be the victim of abusive nagging if the other person is always pressuring you to agree to their wishes on shared decisions or to let them influence decisions that should be yours to make. Nagging is a common tactic in narcissistic parenting but is also used by narcissists in other types of relationships.

Ignoring

Ignoring or shunning is another type of negative reinforcement. This includes "the silent treatment," withholding affection, and so on. It can be as overt as simply refusing to speak to you or acknowledge your presence, or as covert as a vague but persistent atmosphere of emotional coldness and rejection.

Ignoring goes hand in hand with love bombing even though the two may seem to be opposites. First, the abuser gives you the addictive drug of intense affection and admiration—then, she cuts it off completely if you don't do what she wants. Desperate to get the feelings back, you quickly cave in under pressure—and the abuser gains more control.

Some narcissists will alternate positive reinforcement and negative reinforcement just to leave you off-balance and emotionally dependent. This tactic is known as intermittent reinforcement. Through acting cold and dismissive one moment and extremely sweet the next, the abuser creates a situation where the victim is constantly chasing after them and trying to win their approval and affection back.

When the abuser starts being sweet again after ignoring or being cold to you, the relief can be so intense that you actually crave their affection even more than before. This is one example of trauma bonding, where the abuse brings you closer to the abuser in a profoundly toxic way.

Punishment

Ignoring and nagging can both used as types of punishment, along with other behaviors such as yelling, swearing at you, or dramatic emotional displays. By flipping out and making a huge scene when you don't do what he wants, the abuser makes you reluctant to go against his wishes in the future.

One of the most dramatic and frightening types of punishment is "narcissistic rage," where the narcissist responds with total fury to even the slightest hint of criticism. The narcissist may lash out with intentionally vicious personal attacks, escalating in some cases to property destruction or physical violence.

Narcissistic rage has two sides to it. On the one hand, the narcissist's self-image is a fragile veneer covering a much more profound self-loathing. Any criticism destroys the illusion, forcing the narcissist to confront the intolerably painful reality. To this extent, the rage is real.

On the other hand, the narcissist uses her rage to intimidate and manipulate the victim, by creating such a horrible scene that the victim will feel very reluctant ever to criticize the narcissist again. From this perspective, narcissistic rage is just a tactic of manipulation and control.

Sobbing, playing the victim, and threats of self-harm can also be used as forms of punishment. It can be hard to tell whether a person is intentionally trying to punish you or is simply feeling emotional. As always, the key is to see if there is an ongoing pattern. If there is a heavy price tag whenever you fail to do what the other person wants, then it's probably safest to assume they're doing it intentionally.

Guilt Tripping

The guilt trip is one type of punishment behavior. This behavior is especially common when dealing with a narcissistic parent, but it can also be found in other relationships.

The person who is trying to guilt-trip you accuses you of not really loving them, not caring about their problems, or of having done something to harm them in the past. Once they can see that you are feeling guilty, they give you the chance to be absolved of your guilt, but only if you do what they want. For instance, a narcissistic parent may guilt trip you into spending time with them instead of a friend, which also has the effect of isolating you.

Guilt-tripping only works on a person who cares about being loving and kind. It's painful to be told that you aren't a good person, so you're strongly motivated to do whatever it takes to avoid that. Unfortunately, this makes you vulnerable to manipulation.

Of course, if you were really such a terrible and uncaring person, then no one could make you feel guilty in the first place because you just wouldn't care. If someone wants you to feel like a bad person, you should ask yourself what they want from you. If it's something you wouldn't normally do, then they may simply be trying to use your guilt to get past your healthy boundaries and gain control over your decisions.

Emotional Blackmail Tactics

There are four different types of emotional blackmail tactics, as identified by the therapists Forward and Frazier in their study of the topic.

The first type is the threat of punishment, which includes several of the other tactics discussed in this chapter. For example, "Have sex with me, or I'll give you the silent treatment for the next three days," or "Add my name to your bank account, or I'll call off our engagement." The threat of punishment doesn't have to be explicitly stated; it can just as easily be implied.

The second type of emotional blackmail is the threat of self-harm. This is also a type of guilt trip because the obvious implication is that you are responsible for what happens next. "If you break up with me, I'll kill myself" is the clearest example of this tactic.

The third type of emotional blackmail is based on a display of self-pity. This is another type of guilt trip, in which the abuser does something nice for you but makes a big deal about the huge sacrifice they're making. For example, "I cooked you your favorite dinner even though

I have a terrible headache." The idea is to put you in their debt so they can have more leverage over you.

The fourth type of emotional blackmail is to imply that you'll get a reward of some kind if you do whatever the other person wants you to do. This is different from a straightforward exchange of favors because it's used to pressure you into doing something you don't really want to do. In one way or another, it doesn't feel like an equal exchange.

Emotional blackmail tactics can be used for different purposes. Sometimes, they are used to get you to do something little that you might easily have agreed to anyway. Sometimes, they are used to get you to agree to something you're uncomfortable with, but that is still fairly minor in the big scheme of things. Sometimes, they are used to influence your life decisions, such as where to live or whether to go to school. In the most extreme scenario, emotional blackmail can even be used to convince you to participate in criminal behavior.

Isolation Tactics

The narcissistic abuser may use any of these manipulation and control tactics to isolate you from the other people in your life. For example, if you make plans to see a friend for coffee, a narcissistic partner may nag you to change your plans, or give you the silent treatment when you get home or accuse you of not wanting to spend any time with him. He may use emotional blackmail, saying, "Of course I don't mind if you go out with your friends, all I want is for you to be happy. It's just that I've been feeling so depressed."

Whatever specific tactic the narcissist uses, the end result is the same—you find it so difficult to make plans with your friends that you gradually stop doing so, and the narcissist increasingly becomes your only source of emotional support. This not only makes it less likely that you will decide to leave, but it also feeds into the narcissist's own need to be the center of your world.

Mind Games

Abusers often play mind games to keep their victims disoriented and passive. For example, an abuser may set you up to fail by giving you a task without the time or resources needed to complete it successfully. If you accomplish something you're proud of, the abuser may minimize it or refuse to acknowledge it. The abuser may repeatedly remind you of past failures or mistakes, or he may "shift the goalposts" so you're always trying to catch up with an ever-changing set of expectations. He may use a one-sided story about your relationship as a type of propaganda, leading you to accept a distorted view of past events. This is also a type of brainwashing, where the abuser seeks to alter your ability to process reality and form your own opinions about it.

Gaslighting

If you bring up issues in the relationship or things that have hurt your feelings, the abuser may try to convince you that you are simply irrational and that your concerns have no validity. This is known as "gaslighting," the process of making someone doubt their own experiences and memories so they will not question or attempt to resist abuse.

For example, a narcissist who's cheating on you may try to convince you that you are irrationally jealous and controlling. A narcissist who is keeping you isolated may try to convince you that you are a paranoid and suspicious person. Gaslighting tactics are meant to make you feel crazy, so you attribute your legitimate concerns about the relationship to your own mental health issues rather than the other person's behavior.

Blaming the Victim

Gaslighting often goes hand in hand with blaming the victim. The abuser may accuse you of abusing them, or of somehow provoking their abusive behavior. The most common form of "blaming the victim" is seen in cases of domestic violence, where a partner hits you but then blames you for making them so angry in the first place.

In some cases, the narcissist can even convince other people that they really have been wronged and that their victim is "the real abuser." The narcissist's superficial charm can sometimes fool people, leading them to accept a twisted and one-sided interpretation of events. These people can then be manipulated into siding with the narcissist or participating in a smear campaign against the victim of the narcissist's abuse. Victims have coined the phrase "flying monkeys" to describe people who have been manipulated into helping a narcissistic abuser, just like the flying monkey soldiers of the wicked witch in *The Wizard of Oz*.

The Big Picture

Some actions are clearly and unambiguously abusive, such as hitting the other person. Far more often, a toxic relationship has many complex aspects to it, and it's not so easy to say whether a partner is intentionally unmannerly or not.

The big picture is what really matters. Abuse isn't about being passive-aggressive or guilt-trippy on a few occasions—it's an ongoing pattern of control and manipulation. The narcissist isn't just acting out in a moment of weakness but using you as a means to an end. That end is a deep need that can never be satisfied, and the roots of that need to go back to childhood.

Chapter 3: Why Are Some People Narcissistic?

Although there is no way to be certain why some people are narcissistic (while some are not), Narcissistic Personality Disorder is often associated with traumatic experiences in early childhood. Trauma and abuse seem to cause some children to get stuck psychologically, failing to progress from the early and more self-centered stages of development.

All infants are naturally narcissistic in the sense that they care only about their own needs and are unaware that other people exist separately from themselves. Experts in child psychology believe that newborns initially perceive themselves as omnipotent and unlimited by anything, despite the fact that they are completely dependent on others for all their needs.

Why would a powerless infant think of herself as limitlessly powerful? The newborn can't tell the difference at first between herself and other people. Whenever she needs something, her parents or other caregivers immediately and unfailingly provide what she needs. To a newborn infant, the caregiver seems like an extension of the self, an instrument of her own will. Sigmund Freud referred to this as "primary narcissism," the natural and healthy narcissism of the newborn baby.

As the infant develops, she slowly discovers that her needs will not always be met instantly. She sometimes has to cry for a while before anyone picks her up or feeds her, but she learns that she can still rely on them to meet her needs consistently. Over time, she comes to realize that her caregivers are separate individuals rather than extensions of herself and that she is not really omnipotent or unlimited. Infantile narcissism develops into an understanding of human relationships based on affection, boundaries, and mutual trust.

Unfortunately, this process doesn't always work out the way it is supposed to. If the infant's needs aren't consistently met, trust, and a sense of healthy boundaries never get the chance to develop. Instead, the powerful self-centeredness of the newborn remains, along with a deep and painful sense of distrust, insecurity, and anxiety.

Healthy Ego

Some psychologists speak in terms of "healthy narcissism" and "destructive narcissism," while others prefer to use the word "narcissism" exclusively for the destructive manifestation of an unhealthy ego. Either way, a healthy sense of self is very different from the toxic and basically false self of the destructive narcissist.

A person with a healthy ego is self-confident, but his self-confidence is consistent with reality and his own place in the world. The narcissist is not just self-confident but grandiose, seeing himself as unique and special compared to other people. He may even believe that normal social rules apply to other people but not to him, or that there should be no reasonable limits on what he can demand from others.

A person with a healthy ego might be comfortable with power and may even enjoy it, but a narcissist sees power as the most important goal in life and will pursue power over others even if it harms them. His ability to empathize with other people is limited or nonexistent, and he relates to other people primarily as objects.

A person with a healthy ego genuinely cares about other people and respects their basic autonomy. A narcissist will express care for others if it seems like the right thing to say at the time but does not respect their autonomy and will take advantage of them without caring how they might be affected.

A person with healthy ego development has a sense of personal values and can follow through with long-term plans. A narcissist has no underlying sense of values and finds it difficult to stay focused on any one thing for long because he gets bored and distracted so easily.

Finally, a person with healthy ego development is usually someone who experienced a balanced combination of support and boundaries in childhood. Most narcissists experienced some combination of childhood damage to their self-esteem along with a lack of appropriate limits or boundaries between self and other.

The narcissist's inner self is basically stunted, trapped in an early stage of development. He wants to hold on to the newborn's illusion of being unlimited and omnipotent but doesn't trust other people to meet his needs unless he can control and manipulate them into doing so. He doesn't really think of other people as separate from himself but sees them as tools for getting his own needs met. Without a healthy sense of self, he can only avoid facing the reality of his situation by controlling others.

The most common cause for this failure to completely develop is neglect and abuse, often at the hands of a narcissistic parent.

Narcissistic Parenting

Narcissistic parents don't treat their children as unique individuals but as extensions of their own self-image. For a narcissist, the child's absolute trust and dependence on the caregiver make them the perfect source of narcissistic supply—that is, until the child begins to develop into an independent person. This is already a difficult task for the child of a narcissistic parent, who may never have experienced the combination of trust and healthy boundaries needed for healthy ego development. Still, most children will begin to develop a sense of self over time despite these barriers.

This is something the narcissist simply cannot allow, so the narcissistic parent interferes with the child's independent development to keep the child dependent on them. Through guilt-tripping, emotional blackmail, undermining, and all the other techniques of control and manipulation, the narcissistic parent prevents the child from ever really growing up.

The narcissistic parent will often pressure the child to get good grades or excel in sports or impress others in some way. Affection and praise depend on high performance and are withheld as a punishment for any mistake. This is because the narcissistic parent sees the child as an expression of his own ideal self, but it can cause the child to see love and affection solely in terms of external validation. Without the experience of being loved for his own sake, the child of narcissistic parents can develop an unhealthy fixation on how other people perceive him.

Narcissistic parents insist on being the center of their children's lives. At the same time, they often belittle and undermine their children, especially for not living up to their own unrealistic expectations. Over time, the child can learn that the only way to get praise and affection from others is to do just what they want at all times without question. They can just as easily learn that the most effective way to deal with others is through guilt-tripping, manipulation, and other head games.

In effect, the narcissistic parent trains the child to perceive the world and human relationships in a dysfunctional way. This doesn't always turn the child into another narcissist, but it is almost always profoundly damaging to the child's self-esteem.

Effects on the Child

Different children react differently to narcissistic parenting, due to differences in individual temperament as well as the presence of other influences in the child's life. For example, the child may be exposed to examples of loving families and healthy relationships outside the home or may have a healthier relationship with one parent than the other. The child may experience emotional support and affection from some other source, leading them to recognize that something is fundamentally wrong with the type of parenting they get from the narcissist.

For whatever reason, many children of narcissistic parents grow up as kind and empathetic people, though they may experience other problems due to their traumatic childhood. However, many children of narcissistic parents do go on to become narcissists as well, creating a cycle that can extend across multiple generations.

In some cases, the child never develops the sense of trust and stable affection most people experience in infancy. Instead, he experiences the world as a place where even the most important caregivers cannot be counted on. The child may grow up to feel empty inside, fearful and insecure in relationships with others, and unable to develop a clear identity of his own.

In an attempt to fill this sense of emptiness and earn love and affection, the child may repress her own feelings and her own needs to concentrate solely on pleasing the narcissistic parent. The child's underlying resentment and anger about the situation are pushed down beneath a pleasing façade, to come out later in other ways.

This façade or mask can become habitual, a "false self" based on what the other person wants to see. The true self underneath is filled with anger and self-hatred, because the child has never been loved for his own sake and believes himself to be unlovable. Over time, he learns to mirror the grandiose and unrealistic self-image of the narcissistic parent, as well as the behaviors of control and manipulation that allow the narcissist to protect and maintain the false self like a suit of armor.

Although narcissistic abuse in childhood is a frequent cause of narcissism, some people may develop into narcissistic adults without necessarily having been abused.

Parenting Styles

According to counselor Diana Baumrind, parenting styles can be divided into three general categories.

Authoritative parents have high expectations for their children, but they also treat them with love and warmth and are generally responsive to their needs. This parenting style is a healthy balance of love and strictness.

Authoritarian parents have high expectations but treat their children without much warmth and are not particularly responsive to their needs. This may seem similar to narcissistic abuse, but Baumrind's parenting typology was intended as a description of normal parenting variations, not abusive extremes. The authoritarian parenting style is demanding and somewhat cold, but not extreme enough to be considered abusive.

Indulgent or permissive parents don't set high expectations for their children. They don't do much to monitor their child's behavior or correct faults instead of giving the child the freedom to develop on his own. Unfortunately, this includes tolerating rude behaviors such as nagging and being selfish, childish traits that can be described as narcissistic. An authoritative or authoritarian parent wouldn't tolerate that kind of behavior, but the permissive parent prefers to ignore it.

Studies have shown the authoritative style to be the most effective style of parenting overall. Children with authoritative parents tend to be more successful and happy in life than children with either authoritarian or permissive parents, who are more likely to suffer from mental health problems and to abuse alcohol and other substances.

Some experts in child psychology have added a fourth parenting style to this list: the "neglectful" style.

Neglectful parents are similar to permissive parents in that they fail to set consistent boundaries, but different in that they do not offer the child much warmth or affection. In this version of the list, authoritative and permissive parents are affectionate and warm, but authoritative parents also set standards and boundaries more effectively. Authoritarian and neglectful parents are both relatively cold or distant, but neglectful parents also fail to establish limits or boundaries.

According to a research study by Carrie Henschel in *Behavioral Health*, the permissive and authoritarian parenting styles were both associated with narcissism in children. Henschel speculated that permissive parents might encourage narcissism by failing to set healthy limits and letting the child get away with demanding and rude behavior. In addition, permissive parents were more likely to praise a child effusively or describe her as "special" regardless of her actual achievements. The combination of being praised as special without really doing anything and not being corrected for mistreating others could be enough to create the grandiose but shallow self-image of the typical narcissist.

Henschel also found that the authoritarian parenting style could produce narcissistic traits in children. Considering the similarity between the high expectations and low warmth of the authoritarian parenting style and the behavior of a narcissistic parent, it makes sense that authoritarian parenting could also tend to encourage narcissism. However, the authoritarian parent's relative coldness is not as extreme and doesn't include the manipulative head games of the narcissistic parent.

Henschel didn't consider the effects of neglectful parenting, but some of the permissive parents in her study might have fallen under that category as well since it was added to the list as a variation on the permissive style. It's easy to see how an emotionally distant parenting style could contribute to narcissism in the child, especially when combined with a lack of boundaries and limits. Children learn how to care for others when their parents care for them, and they learn how to respect boundaries when their parents set limits on acceptable behavior. A child of neglectful parents might not have the opportunity to learn either empathy or respect for boundaries.

Narcissistic Entitlement

Henschel's research into permissive parenting might explain one of the most frustrating aspects of narcissistic behavior—the narcissist's seemingly endless sense of entitlement.

According to narcissistic abuse expert Melanie Tonia Evans, the narcissist feels entitled to get whatever he wants whenever he wants it and perceives any refusal to give him what he wants as a horrible injustice. This can include anything from attention to affection to money to sex—there are no legitimate limits on what he has the right to expect from other people in the eyes of the narcissist. Even though the narcissist treats others as if they have no rights, he expects others to respect his rights at all times.

Evans traces this colossal sense of entitlement to four separate causes, any one of which can produce a narcissist. The first is abuse and neglect, such as the experience of being raised by a narcissistic parent. The second is being raised by overly permissive parents who fail to establish boundaries and never say no. The third is being raised by overly indulgent parents who try too hard to give the child everything he could ever want. The fourth is being raised by parents who put the child on a pedestal, creating an overblown but basically fragile sense of self-worth. The child ends up perceiving herself as being special and better than others, entitled to anything she wants just like Violet Beauregarde in *Charlie and the Chocolate Factory*.

As Evans pointed out, the act of putting your child on a pedestal like this is also narcissistic, as the child is treated as an extension of the parents' ego. This suggests that parental narcissism may be a factor even when the parent isn't actually abusive. The narcissistic parent uses the child to prop up his own false self and influences the child to see the world in the same way.

Other Factors

Other factors may also contribute to the development of a narcissistic personality. Researchers have found some physical differences between the brains of people diagnosed with narcissistic personality disorder and other people. Narcissistic people seem to have less gray matter in two areas of the brain: the prefrontal cortex and the left anterior insula.

These areas of the brain are associated with the ability to experience empathy for others as well as the ability to regulate emotion. This implies that people with a narcissistic personality disorder may have difficulty keeping their own emotions from spiraling out of control and may also find it hard to empathize with other people's feelings. Quick to feel anger or anxiety and slow to feel empathy, the narcissist may simply be at the mercy of her own emotions.

Of course, it's difficult to say whether these brain differences really cause narcissistic personality disorder or whether they are just one factor among many. For example, having less gray matter in your left anterior insula might not make you narcissistic on its own, but might make you more likely to become narcissistic with the right life experiences. As with many other mental health problems, a narcissistic personality disorder may be caused by a combination of environmental and genetic factors.

Problems Associated with Narcissism

Narcissism tends to go along with other mental health problems and personality disorders. People diagnosed with NPD often suffer from depression. They are also more likely to be diagnosed with Bipolar Disorder, also known as manic depression. The person suffering from Bipolar Disorder will alternate between extremely depressed and manically energetic moods.

People with NPD have high rates of substance abuse issues and are especially likely to abuse cocaine. They have high rates of anorexia and may also have higher rates of other personality disorders, including Borderline, Anti-Social, and Paranoid disorders.

Narcissism is so strongly associated with other mental health issues that counselors usually make a diagnosis of NPD after the patient comes in for some other reason. For example, the narcissist may seek treatment for depression after a breakup caused by his own narcissistic behavior, without any insight into his own role in the breakdown of the relationship. Even though he can tell that something is wrong, he still believes the other person mistreated him rather than the other way around.

Although the narcissist is deeply unhappy and incapable of forming healthy relationships with others, most narcissists are unwilling and unable to see themselves as the problem. Seeking help for narcissism would mean admitting that the narcissist's ideal self is actually fake. Because the narcissist can't bear to do this, he blames everyone else for his problems instead.

The therapist who realizes her patient is narcissistic may make a diagnosis of NPD but will have a hard time making any progress as long as the narcissist continues to cling to the false self. Narcissists in treatment are known for arguing with their therapists, and being stubborn about treatment, impervious to any argument the therapist may present.

Chapter 4: How Narcissists Think

Now that we've examined why some people become narcissists in the first place, we can begin to explore how narcissists think. The starting point for any examination of the narcissist should always be the *Diagnostic and Statistical Manual of Mental Disorders* or *DSM*—the book that therapists use to diagnose their clients. In the *DSM*, Narcissistic Personality Disorder is defined as a pattern of grandiose behavior and/or fantasy combined with a lack of empathy and a need to be admired by others. As with any other personality disorder, narcissism would not be diagnosed unless it was interfering with the person's ability to live a healthy and happy life.

A counselor can make a diagnosis of Narcissistic Personality Disorder for any person who presents at least five of the disorder's nine known characteristics:

- An excessive sense of self-importance or grandiosity
- Fantasizing obsessively about limitless power, beauty, brilliance, success, or idealized love
- A belief that one is unique or special

- Requiring high levels of admiration from others
- An entitled mentality
- A tendency to exploit other people
- An inability to show empathy for others
- A strong tendency toward envy
- An arrogant or conceited attitude

Because diagnosis can be made without all nine symptoms being present, you shouldn't assume that the absence of anyone's symptom means that the person is not really a narcissist. For example, the person you suspect of being a narcissist may not seem all that envious of others, but may still be arrogant, unempathetic, exploitative, entitled, and self-important. Of course, only a professional can officially diagnose someone with NPD.

We can add to this list of nine symptoms the widely used concept of the false self or ideal self, the mask the narcissist wears to keep the vulnerable inner self or true self from being exposed. The need to hide the true self and prop up the false self is what drives the narcissist to exploit other people as sources of "narcissistic supply," first idealizing them and then cruelly devaluing them in the cycle of narcissistic abuse.

Types of Narcissists

Not all narcissists are exactly the same. There are a number of subtypes, although researchers have not yet settled on a complete list. Some of these subtypes include:

- The normal or "pure" narcissist without other complicating factors
- The unprincipled narcissist, who shares a lot in common with the antisocial personality type
- The amorous or seductive narcissist
- The elitist narcissist, who seems himself as part of an inherently superior group of people
- The compensatory narcissist, who is primarily motivated by feelings of inferiority
- The hedonistic narcissist, who tends to procrastinate and dodge responsibility
- The fanatic narcissist, motivated by paranoid yet grandiose fantasies
- The spiritual narcissist, who uses meditation or religion to manipulate others
- The malignant narcissist, driven by paranoia, sadism, and the need for revenge

Although researchers have developed these subtypes to help them understand how narcissists think, few narcissists would fit perfectly into just one category and the subtypes are not included in the DSM. You should think of them as convenient tools for understanding the narcissist's inner drives and motivations, but not as rigid categories. A fanatic narcissist might show some of the same behaviors as a malignant narcissist, or an amorous narcissist might also seem elitist or compensatory.

The Normal Narcissist

The "normal" narcissist isn't exactly normal but is closer to normal behavior than the other types of a narcissist. A normal narcissist still thinks of himself as being unique and special, and still acts entitled in his relationships with other people. He expects other people to recognize and admire his talents, and he may actually be talented in leadership roles. He has a tendency to be competitive, ambitious, and bold. However, his interactions with others often lack fairness, equality, or reciprocity. Because the normal narcissist's issues are not as severe or complex as other types of a narcissist, he may be able to show some empathy and concern for other people even if his level of empathy is below normal. This category is similar but not identical to the concept of the "pure narcissist," meaning a narcissist without any additional personality disorders or mental health problems to complicate his symptoms. The normal narcissist is still a problem to deal with, but arguably less of a problem than most of the other types. He wants to win and to be admired, and he has a hard time giving other people as much as he expects them to give him—but he isn't necessarily compelled to hurt them.

The Unprincipled Narcissist

The unprincipled narcissist is a con artist and seeks to gain an advantage over other people through fraud and guile. Unprincipled narcissists lack a normal conscience and combine the narcissist's exploitative and arrogant nature with a criminal's willingness to deceive others for personal gain. The unprincipled narcissist has some of the features of Anti-Social Personality Disorder, the formal diagnosis for sociopaths and psychopaths. People with ASPD have a pattern of hurting other people or violating their rights in some way without showing remorse. They tend to get in trouble with the law and to be violent and aggressive, with a hard and uncaring attitude to the people they hurt. Although unprincipled narcissists have a similar mindset, including a tendency to disregard the rules of society, they often avoid crossing the line into outright criminality. However, their behavior toward others is still amoral and self-serving, and they sometimes end up in trouble with the law as a result. The unprincipled narcissist sees other people as suckers who deserve to be used and exploited, then cast aside. Their superficial charm often prevents other people from recognizing their true nature, which is basically hostile and contemptuous. If anyone sees them for what they are and gets in the way, they tend to be highly vindictive. Unprincipled narcissists have no concept of loyalty, so they will typically move from one victim to the next throughout their lives, seeing each new person as just another fool to be fleeced.

The Amorous Narcissist

The amorous narcissist is a seducer, and his main source of narcissistic supply comes from new sexual and romantic conquests. Just as the unprincipled narcissist shares some features of ASPD, the amorous narcissist has symptoms in common with Histrionic Personality Disorder. This disorder is characterized by a constant need for attention and approval, which is usually gained through seductive behavior and dramatic emotional displays. Like a person with Histrionic Personality Disorder, the amorous narcissist pursues one affair after another but is unlikely to commit to any of his lovers since real intimacy is not what he wants. Amorous narcissists are especially charming and flirtatious because they are always seeking a new source of the attention and approval they crave. They lie easily and frequently. Amorous narcissists like to think of themselves as excellent lovers but are focused solely on physical performance rather than emotional connection. They often withdraw immediately after sex, because they don't have any interest in other aspects of romance. Some amorous narcissists also belittle and undermine their partners verbally to gain more control over them, but not all amorous narcissists seem to share this trait. Amorous narcissists will use guilt trips and emotional blackmail to pressure their partners into having sex. Some studies have also shown a link between amorous narcissism in men and violent tendencies.

The Elitist Narcissist

The elitist narcissist is likely to come from a relatively privileged socioeconomic background or at least to see herself that way. Elitists narcissists are social climbers and always want to be seen as having some connection to rich, famous, or powerful people or institutions. They take a grandiose pride in achievements that don't really amount to much or are far less impressive than they want to believe. The elitist narcissist may have been raised as a "golden child"—indulged and praised by permissive parents and treated as special without having done anything to earn such praise. The elitist narcissist is basically a variation on the "normal" or "pure" narcissist. Their source of narcissistic supply is their perceived elite status, and they always want to be seen as the winner in every situation. They have a poor understanding of boundaries and limits and are constantly looking for ways to move up in the world. However, their illusion of elite status is more likely to be based on who they know than on anything they've actually done. They crave reflected glory.

The Compensatory Narcissist

Although all narcissists can be described as having a true self and a false self, this trait is especially marked in the compensatory narcissist. The compensatory narcissist is more intensely aware of her own feelings of inferiority and shame and is driven to compensate for these feelings by presenting herself as superior to others. Compensatory narcissism has characteristics in common with both Passive-Aggressive Personality Disorder and Avoidant Personality Disorder, including both manipulative, passive-aggressive behavior, and extreme social anxiety. Compensatory narcissists are not social butterflies like amorous narcissists. Instead, they are more likely to isolate themselves to avoid dealing with the contradiction between their grandiose self-image and the painful self-doubt they constantly experience.

The Hedonistic Narcissist

The hedonistic narcissist shows a mix of traits from the normal, unprincipled, amorous, elitist, and compensatory narcissistic subtypes. Hedonistic narcissists seek out pleasure and avoid responsibility and show a strong tendency to self-deception. They prefer to avoid conflict whenever possible and are highly sensitive to perceived rejection. They also tend to be under-motivated and passive, procrastinating important tasks or sabotaging their own success in other ways. When confronted on any topic, the hedonistic narcissist will deflect blame for his actions onto other people. Hedonistic narcissists are known for brooding and introspection, which can sometimes develop into an elaborate fantasy life for them to retreat into.

The Fanatic Narcissist

The fanatic narcissist is a narcissist with a mission, which can be anything from saving the world to taking grandiose revenge on those who have harmed him. The false self of the fanatic narcissist is a savior fantasy—he wants to be seen as a great leader of some kind. Depending on the mission he decides to focus on, the fanatic narcissist may present himself as a saint, mystic, revolutionary, visionary, inventor, or prophet. Fanatic narcissism is basically narcissism with features of Paranoid Personality Disorder, and the fanatic narcissist will frequently express paranoid distrust and suspicion of others. This type of narcissist is openly pretentious and arrogant toward other people, seeing them as in need of his supposedly benevolent guidance and leadership. Numerous studies have described narcissism as a defining personality trait of the violent terrorist, who seeks to cleanse or purify society through acts of spectacular cruelty in the name of an inflexible ideology. However, not all fanatic narcissists or focused on political or religious causes, and not all of them are physically violent. The defining feature of fanatic narcissism is simply the grandiose yet overblown sense of having a special mission to fulfill.

The Spiritual Narcissist

The spiritual narcissist may be considered a subtype of the fanatic narcissist. This type of narcissist lives in a fantasy world of pseudo-spirituality, using spiritual teachings in a distorted and out-of-context way to control and manipulate other people. For example, the spiritual narcissist may do something harmful to your self-esteem, but then tell you he is just teaching you to overcome your ego and bring you closer to enlightenment. The spiritual narcissist isn't really spiritual at all, but he uses teachings from Buddhism or Taoism or Christianity to justify his persistent misuse of other people.

The Malignant Narcissist

The malignant narcissist is possibly the most destructive and dangerous type of narcissist. Malignant narcissism is not merely narcissism, but a combination of the

Narcissistic, Anti-Social, Sadistic, and Paranoid personality disorders.

No matter how deficient in empathy that the average narcissist may possibly be, most of them are only seeking to meet their own need for approval and recognition. They often harm others in the process, but harming others is not usually the point of what they are doing. The idealized self of the malignant narcissist is based on fantasies of power, cruelty, and aggression, so harming other people is precisely the point. Where a normal narcissist would have a diminished ability to feel remorse for the pain they cause, the malignant narcissist takes sadistic delight in causing pain.

Paranoia is also a major feature of this subtype. Malignant narcissists project their own negative feelings and trauma experiences on everyone else they interact with, constantly acting out the fantasy of being a larger-than-life figure of grandiose aggression and violence. Malignant narcissists are highly dangerous individuals and often end up committing major crimes.

Even when a malignant narcissist's actions have not yet crossed the line into physical violence, they are still generally characterized by hostility and cruelty. Malignant narcissists take offense very easily and will try to psychologically destroy anyone they perceive as having harmed or insulted them. This extends even into petty daily interactions—for instance, a malignant narcissist may say something intentionally hurtful as revenge for disagreeing with him about some minor issue. This is an expression of the malignant narcissist's paranoia. He sees even a hint of criticism as a personal attack and responds in kind.

Malignant narcissists also tend to see everything in stark black-and-white terms. Everyone is either a winner or a loser, and he intends to be a winner. Everyone is either powerful or powerless, and he intends to be powerful. In the mind of the malignant narcissist, the only alternative to vicious cruelty is a pathetic weakness.

Grandiose or Vulnerable?

Unsurprisingly, there is a lot of overlap between all these subtypes of narcissism, and it may not always be easy to say which category a particular narcissist fits into. Some mental health counselors use a much simpler system in which there are only two subtypes: the grandiose narcissist and the vulnerable narcissist.

Grandiose narcissists fit the stereotype of being extroverted, superficially charming, and larger-than-life. Vulnerable narcissists are shy and introverted, yet ultimately display the same self-centered and manipulative traits in their interactions with others.

The normal, unprincipled, elitist, fanatic and malignant subtypes would probably fit under the grandiose category, while the compensatory and hedonistic subtypes might fit more easily in the vulnerable category.

The vulnerable or "covert introvert" narcissist doesn't display the same obvious traits as the grandiose narcissist. Instead of seeking attention, the covert narcissist keeps to herself more. However, the underlying narcissism of her mentality still comes out in different ways.

Covert narcissists tend to be judgmental and highly critical of others, but this attitude is most likely to be expressed in subtle ways. They are often described as smug or passive-aggressive, and they may express disdain for others by rolling their eyes or acting bored and distracted when other people are talking.

They give the impression of being self-absorbed and may show their basic lack of empathy through inappropriate requests. For example, a covert narcissist may expect you to do a favor for them even though you just told them you were feeling sick. When you need something from them, they might agree but then never follow through, or they might act passive-aggressive in other ways. If you confront them about this behavior, they may respond by giving you the silent treatment or otherwise withdrawing from the interaction.

Just like other types of a narcissist, the covert or vulnerable narcissist sees himself as being special and superior to others. He may describe himself as being misunderstood or uniquely intelligent and talented compared to other people. The mindset of the covert narcissist isn't fundamentally different from that of any other narcissist, but the quiet approach and lack of extroversion can make them harder to recognize.

How to Know If You're a Narcissist

Narcissists are not usually very good at recognizing themselves, but if you have any suspicion that you might be a narcissist, then this checklist should help you figure it out.

- Do you interrupt other people while they're talking?
- Do you find your mind wandering when other people are talking?
- Do you find yourself getting impatient often?
- Do you consider yourself charming?
- Are you highly competitive?
- Do you put new romantic partners on a pedestal?
- Do you find yourself criticizing or belittling other people in your life when they irritate you?
- Do you hold grudges or come up with revenge schemes when you feel wronged or insulted?
- Do you often give people advice when they haven't asked you to do so?
- Do you frequently feel the need to be the center of attention at parties or meetings?
- Do you feel reluctant to say sorry or admit to being wrong?

- Do you attribute your own actions to being provoked by other people?
- Have other people accused you of taking advantage of them?
- Do you see your relationships primarily in terms of what they can do for you?
- Do you struggle with addiction to alcohol, drugs, gambling, or sex?
- Do you see yourself as unusually intelligent, talented, or unique?
- Do you see yourself as being destined to do great things?

No one can diagnose you with Narcissistic Personality Disorder except a qualified mental health professional, but if you answered "yes" to a lot of these questions, then you should consider the possibility that you have some narcissistic traits. A professional might be able to help you assess the situation and determine if you need to make some changes in your life to be happier and have better relationships with other people. Plenty of people have some narcissistic qualities without being full-blown narcissists and seeking help doesn't mean you have a personality disorder.

You can also use this checklist to help you figure out whether someone else in your life is a narcissist. Even if you don't think you're the victim of narcissistic abuse, it can still be helpful to spot the potential narcissists in your life so you can be on your guard. Little details like a habit of monopolizing attention might not seem too important until you begin to see them as part of a broader pattern.

Chapter 5: Who Do Narcissists Target?

The narcissist rarely has trouble drawing people in, but the reason for this is not solely due to the narcissist's own charm. In fact, some people are much more vulnerable to narcissistic abuse than others. Narcissists are skilled at recognizing and targeting these people. If you learn what the narcissist is looking for in a potential victim, you'll have a much better chance of keeping yourself safe from narcissistic abuse in the future.

The prime characteristic the narcissist is looking for is codependency, the self-destructive urge to take a caregiver role even if it harms you. Narcissists sometimes get in relationships with other narcissists, but more often than not a narcissist will partner with a codependent person.

Oddly enough, the main cause of codependency is childhood trauma, which is also the main cause of narcissism. In fact, the two conditions are broadly similar and can be interpreted as different attempts to solve the same underlying problem. A child who cannot develop a stable sense of self looks for the self in the reactions of others. Narcissism and codependency are two different ways of doing that.

One child in a dysfunctional family may develop traits of narcissism while another develops the symptoms of codependency. In both cases, the child was unable to develop a healthy sense of self because of the dysfunctional family situation, but one child responded by craving validation from others and became a narcissist, while the other responded by trying to take care of everyone and became codependent.

Later in life, the narcissist keeps looking for new ways to prop up his idealized persona and avoid facing the pain and shame he carries inside. The codependent sibling keeps looking for someone to take care of, someone to subordinate her own needs as well. Oftentimes, the narcissistic sibling will end up in a relationship with a codependent person, and the codependent sibling will end up in a relationship with a narcissist.

Codependent behavior can be described as narcissistic in some circumstances. For instance, a mother who focuses on her children to the exclusion of everything else in her life might be described as codependent, since she defines herself solely by her self-sacrificing caregiver behavior. However, it's easy to use caregiving as a manipulative strategy, especially when combined with guilt-tripping and emotional blackmail, in which case the behavior is essentially narcissistic.

Some therapists consider narcissism to simply be a type of codependency, as the narcissist is just as dependent on the opinions of others and often for the same reasons. It is possible for one person to be narcissistic in some relationships and codependent in others. For example, a mother whose attitude to her children is basically narcissistic can still function as a codependent caregiver to an alcoholic husband. The difference is simply that the codependent person is the giver in the relationship while the narcissist is the taker, yet both parties need each other to play out the roles they feel compelled to play.

The Symptoms of Codependency

Unlike narcissism, codependency is not a diagnosed personality disorder. However, codependency does have a set of recognizable characteristics or symptoms, including:

- Weak boundaries between self and other, a tendency to internalize and take responsibility for other people's emotions
- A deep sense of inner shame or inadequacy
- Poor self-esteem
- Difficulty saying "no," and an urge to please others even when it causes you harm
- A powerful need to take care of someone or a feeling of worthlessness unless other people need you
- Poor communication skills or reluctance to say what you're really feeling
- Inability to clearly articulate your own needs
- Obsessively thinking about and analyzing your relationships with others.
- A tendency to react with intense emotion to any judgment or criticism
- The urge to control other people and make their decisions for them
- Denial of your needs in favor of meeting the needs of others
- Fear of emotional intimacy
- Perfectionism
- Inability to be alone, causing intense depression when you are not in a relationship

- A strong need to be recognized for all your sacrifices, leading to resentment when you don't feel appreciated
- A feeling that you are unworthy of love, or that you are a failure
- Fear of abandonment
- Denial of the problem

To sum up all these characteristics, the codependent person is driven by a deep inner wound to seek for love and validation but believes herself to be unworthy of the love she seeks. This drives her to prove herself through extravagant self-sacrifice, putting the other person's needs above her own. When her self-destructive people-pleasing is not appreciated, she becomes resentful and passive-aggressive. However, she finds it almost impossible to break the relationship off due to her fear of being alone.

In other words, the relationship between a narcissist and a codependent person is not just a simple matter of abuser and victim. The narcissistic abuser needs someone to put him first, and the codependent person needs to put someone first. In theory, these needs could be compatible. However, the narcissist's basic lack of empathy poisons the dynamic. No matter how much self-sacrifice the codependent offers, the narcissist will never reciprocate with gratitude and appreciation. Instead, the narcissist will project his self-loathing onto his codependent partner while remaining self-centered and entitled. The only possible result is misery for both of them.

How Does Codependency Develop?

Role reversal is one of the most common childhood experiences that can cause codependency later in life. Role reversal happens whenever the child is asked to play the role of the parent. If a parent is unable to take care of themselves due to illness, substance abuse, or mental health problems, the child may step in and take over the caregiver role.

Sometimes, this role is basically forced on the child by a dysfunctional parent, but there are also cases where it happens as an unavoidable consequence of a serious illness and a lack of support from outside the household. Either way, it's deeply harmful to a child to take on the parental role. The child often develops a compulsive need to be the caregiver in every relationship, along with intense but buried resentment for having been forced into such a demanding role at such an early age. The martyr-like qualities of the codependent come from this paradoxical combination of resentment and self-sacrificing altruism.

Codependency can also develop from other sources of childhood trauma. For instance, if the child's caregivers fail to offer emotional support when needed, the child can develop a deep sense of being all alone and unsupported. They may feel the need to act out the support they wish they had received when they were young, causing them to develop the compulsive caregiving traits of the codependent.

Some parents discourage their children from expressing any negative emotions, not understanding that children learn how to regulate their emotions by receiving love and care from their parents. Instead of comforting a crying child, they may snap at him or tell him to toughen up. This can cause the child to develop deep feelings of shame about his own emotions and his own vulnerability, which can then develop into either narcissism or codependency as the child tries to find acceptance and support from outside the self through one strategy or the other.

A child who grows up in an abusive household may learn to associate love and approval with successfully pleasing the abusive parent and avoiding their often unpredictable anger. This pattern of self-negation and people-pleasing can develop into codependency if the child retains the capacity for empathy, or it can develop into narcissism if the capacity for empathy is lost. In both cases, the person sees love and acceptance as something that depends on how others perceive you. The difference between the two is that the codependent wants to make the other person happy and thus "earn" love and acceptance, while the narcissist wants to convince the other person that he "deserves" love and acceptance due to his superior qualities.

Children raised in abusive households often develop high levels of empathy, becoming hypersensitive to how other people feel in their attempts to avoid angering an abusive caregiver. The codependent's capacity for empathy protects them from becoming narcissistic. Unfortunately, it also leaves them vulnerable to abuse by narcissists.

The Appeal of the Narcissist

What makes the narcissist so appealing to the codependent person in the first place? It's a combination of factors. The narcissist's apparent self-confidence can make him seem compelling and dynamic. The codependent person lacks a solid inner self, and the narcissist seems to have what she lacks. He actually doesn't, because his impressive persona is only a front. However, the codependent person has no way of knowing this and is drawn to a partner who seems to have what she's missing.

The codependent person is emotionally wounded and searching for someone to give her the unconditional love and positive regard she wasn't able to find as a child. Unfortunately for her, the narcissist's love-bombing tactic looks exactly like the healing and validation she yearns for. It really isn't, because the narcissist is only doing what he has to do to establish a new source of narcissistic supply. Once the relationship is established, the narcissist drops the act and just starts demanding what he feels entitled to.

The codependent's need to serve others will ensure that she supplies the narcissist with what he wants, but the narcissist feels no need to continue supplying the affection and warmth the codependent needs. Every now and then, the narcissist may start love-bombing the codependent again just to keep her from leaving. This is especially likely after the narcissist's abusive and harmful behavior has pushed the codependent almost to the point of walking away. By turning the charm back on for a little while, the narcissist can fool the codependent into thinking things are really getting better—for a little while. The rest of the time, he will simply take advantage, seeing himself as fully entitled to what the codependent offers.

The toxic dynamic between the narcissist and the codependent becomes a cycle of abuse, which can be broken only when the narcissist moves on to a new source of narcissistic supply or when the codependent decides to break the cycle. Few if any narcissists will ever break the cycle on their own.

Narcissistic Friends and Family Members

Because the same family dynamic can just as easily produce either narcissism or codependency, a codependent person is very likely to have one or more narcissistic family members.

In this situation, the narcissist doesn't have to seek out a codependent partner to get access to the narcissistic supply he needs, because he already has that relationship within his own family.

For instance, a narcissistic sibling can exploit a codependent sibling's need to be the caregiver by demanding a constant supply of attention and support through guilt-tripping and emotional blackmail. A narcissistic parent can take advantage of a codependent child by expecting them to be on call at all times while undermining the child's attempts to establish healthy relationships with other people.

These relationships can be just as toxic as any romantic relationship because they're built on the same destructive pattern of exploitation on one side and self-sacrifice on the other.

The same dynamic applies to other situations such as the workplace. A narcissistic coworker will quickly pick up on the codependent's self-negating tendencies and begin to take advantage—first with small requests for favors and minor boundary violations, then progressing to however much exploitation and manipulation the narcissist can get away with.

The narcissist-codependent dynamic also occurs in platonic friendships. The narcissist uses the codependent friend as a limitless source of unconditional affection and support but shows no interest in being there for the codependent friend in the same way. For instance, a narcissistic friend might expect you to pick up the phone every time she wants to vent while changing the topic or acting irritated any time you say anything about your own life.

The narcissistic friend is also likely to disappear whenever she finds a new and more potent source of narcissistic supply. For example, she may call or want to hang out only when she's single but drop out of contact completely whenever she has a boyfriend. The narcissist in this situation is using her friend as a "spare tire," a backup source of narcissistic supply for when she's between relationships.

Enabling

Codependents frequently engage in enabling behavior—that is, behavior that enables the other person to keep doing whatever destructive thing they've been doing without experiencing the consequences of that behavior.

For example, a codependent in a relationship with an alcoholic might clean up after them, call in sick for them, or try to keep other people from realizing how bad the problem really is. While this behavior fulfills the codependent's need to be the caregiver, it also makes it easier for the alcoholic to keep drinking. The concept of codependency was first developed by studying people in recovery for alcoholism, who often have complex enabling relationships with romantic partners and family members. Researchers examining these types of relationships then discovered that codependency is not restricted to alcoholism but occurs in many different dysfunctional relationships.

A codependent person in a relationship with a narcissist might engage in any of the following behaviors:

- Minimizing or excusing the narcissist's abusive behavior
- Keeping the narcissist's destructive actions private
- Taking the blame or consequences for things the narcissist actually did
- Paying debts that the narcissist incurred, such as debts from gambling or misusing credit
- Participating in the abuser's triangulation strategies
- Acting as the abuser's agent or "flying monkey" to re-victimize previous victims
- Helping the narcissist hide criminal or immoral behavior from public knowledge
- Giving the narcissist control over your finances

These behaviors, though driven by the codependent's own need to take care of other people, only make it easier for the narcissist to continue the cycle of abuse and exploitation.

How Do Narcissists Recognize Codependent People?

While the narcissist's ability to find and target a codependent person might seem mysterious, it isn't a sixth sense. The narcissist chooses her target by testing people, then focuses on those who show signs of codependent behavior.

Of course, this isn't how the narcissist sees things at all. In the mind of the narcissist, everything the codependent does for her is simply fair and reasonable. As far as she's concerned, she has every right to it. However, the narcissist still has to find people willing to give her what she thinks she deserves. In practice, that means testing people and seeing what they'll put up with.

The codependent person has an extremely difficult time saying "no" to others because his weak boundaries make it hard for him to tell where his responsibilities begin and end. For example, if the codependent's brother spends the rent money on drugs and alcohol, the codependent feels the need to protect him from the natural consequences of this decision. He feels like he'll be responsible if his brother gets evicted or becomes homeless, even though the problem was caused solely by his own poor decision-making.

The narcissist knows this and will test your reactions early in the relationship to see how good you are at saying "no." If you set healthy boundaries early on, the narcissist will see that you are not an easy target and back off.

This applies not only to unreasonable requests but to other forms of boundary testing. Most people take their time before committing to a serious relationship because they want to get to know the person a bit better before they make any major commitments. Codependent people don't always do this, because they have such a need to take care of someone and to not be alone that they are easily convinced to get involved quickly.

When a narcissist love-bombs you, it's not just a matter of getting swept away or putting you on a pedestal. Those might be factors because the narcissist will typically idealize a new partner for a little while before the devaluation process sets in.

However, love-bombing also functions as a test of how codependent you are. If you go along with it, if the narcissist's over-the-top displays of adoration seem to be something you crave and need, then the narcissist knows you might be codependent.

As you can see, the narcissist's actions in the early stages of the relationship serve several purposes, one of which is to interview you for the position of his next victim. It doesn't really matter if he doesn't see it that way, or if he protests that his love for you is completely sincere. Actions are what really matter, not pretty words.

It's natural to want to help the people you love whenever you can, and it's natural to be excited by a new partner who seems to be falling for you. If they are really sincere, they'll still feel the same way after some time has passed. The best way to avoid being targeted by a narcissist is to set reasonable boundaries and refuse to be blackmailed or pressured into changing your mind. If you know how to say "no," most narcissists will leave you alone and seek an easier target.

If you've just met a new person and you feel like you might be falling in love, don't get so swept away that you allow the relationship to move too quickly. True love won't just evaporate because you take your time, and waiting will prove that the other person's love for you is real and not just a case of love-bombing.

If your potential partner is a narcissist, they're not likely to stick around once you ask them to slow things down a little. In fact, their fragile inner self will often lead them to take it as a personal rejection. They may lash out maliciously or pressure you to change your mind.

If you ask someone new in your life to take things slow or to respect your boundaries, watch how they respond. If they try to emotionally blackmail you by saying something like "don't you really love me?", then you may be dealing with a narcissist. If they say something hurtful, like "you're not really very attractive anyway, I could do better," then you may be dealing with a narcissist.

Chapter 6: Dealing with a Narcissist

Understanding how narcissists think and who they are most likely to target for narcissistic abuse, you are now in a much better position to deal with any narcissists in your life. Whether the narcissist in question is a spouse, romantic partner, family member, friend, or boss, these tips and strategies will help you keep a clear head and respond effectively.

Effective Responses

There are a number of effective responses to narcissistic abuse, but they all have one thing in common: an understanding of what the narcissist really wants. No matter what seems to be happening at the moment, the narcissist is always looking for power. The most effective responses are those which allow you to keep your power rather than giving any more of it away to the narcissist. This means not allowing the narcissist to disregard your boundaries, but it also means not reacting emotionally in ways that might make the narcissist more powerful in the situation.

Clarify Your Boundaries

The first and most important step is to clarify your boundaries. For a codependent person, developing clear boundaries is always difficult. One of the defining characteristics of codependency is a lack of clarity about where the self ends and where others begin, so you may need to clarify that for yourself before you can begin to establish boundaries with the other people in your life. You are not responsible for how other people feel, for what they do, or for the consequences of their actions. You are only ever responsible for your own actions.

To start the process, make a list describing how you want to be treated by the other people in your life. The list should have clear statements about the kind of behavior you aren't willing to tolerate. For example, "no putting me down" or "no guilt-tripping."

Making a list might be a little challenging, especially if your self-esteem is badly damaged or if you've been conditioned to feel that you don't have any rights. If you feel like you're always responsible for other people's emotional reactions, you might feel guilty about setting boundaries.

If this is how you're feeling, remind yourself that you have the same rights as anyone else. First and foremost, you have the right to say, "no." One way to write your list of boundaries is to ask yourself what you wish you could say "no" to. Everything you wish you could say "no" to is a boundary you can set.

For instance, if your mother always calls you on the weekend and asks you to run errands for her no matter what else you had planned, you probably wish you could say no in that situation. The truth is that you can—you just need to establish a clear boundary. Add "not doing errands for Mom without advance notice" to your list of boundaries.

Once you have your list, attach a realistic consequence to each boundary. For example, "if anyone tries to make me feel guilty, I will not do what they are asking me to do," or "if anyone shouts at me, I will leave and go someplace safe."

The consequences should not be retaliation, just basic and logical steps to protect yourself and your own boundaries. For every situation in your life that feels abusive or manipulative, you should have a clearly-defined boundary and a clearly-defined consequence. The goal is to know just what you will do ahead of time, so you don't need to react emotionally when the situation comes up.

Assert Yourself

Asserting yourself is not the same as being aggressive or hostile and is completely different from being passive-aggressive or resentful. In order to assert yourself effectively, it's essential to stay calm. Stand up for yourself but don't let the narcissist push your buttons. He will almost certainly try!

Be as direct as possible. For example, if your partner launches into a tirade about your shortcomings, don't respond with a counterattack or a resentful hint about how you're feeling. Instead, just tell them that you aren't willing to participate in a conversation where you're being put down, then walk away from the conversation.

If someone is trying to guilt-trip you into spending time with them, tell them you aren't available and leave it at that. If they tell you that you don't care about them because of the boundary you're setting, tell them you disagree, or you see it differently.

Whenever you assert yourself, be as clear as possible about what you are willing to do and what you aren't willing to do. Stick to the boundaries you've set and refuse to engage with any attempts to manipulate you.

If the person you're talking to is being abusive, confront what they're doing in the clearest terms. For example, "I don't like it when you call me stupid. If you want to continue this conversation, don't do that again."

To establish clear boundaries may take a little while because the narcissist has to see that you really mean it. He will try to push it, testing to see if your resolve will weaken. Follow through with your consequences every single time, and the narcissist will either learn to respect them or leave the situation.

Projection

Projection is simple if an immature psychological defense mechanism in which negative emotions and self-criticism are projected outward onto another person to avoid having to face them directly. Narcissists use projection all the time because their true or inner self is the complete opposite from the false or ideal self they want others to see.

Whenever anything reminds them of how they really feel inside, they defend themselves by projecting the negative emotion onto another person. When the narcissist is feeling incompetent, he will accuse you of incompetence. When the narcissist is feeling ugly, he will call you ugly. When the narcissist is feeling worthless and unlovable, he will do everything in his power to make you feel worthless and unlovable.

Understanding this process is the key to not being controlled by it. If you have unclear boundaries, it's hard not to absorb what the narcissist is saying. When your boundaries are stronger, you can see that the narcissist isn't really talking about you at all—she's talking about how she feels inside.

You can deal with sniping and minor put-downs by refusing to react the way the narcissist is hoping for. The narcissist is always looking for an emotional response because no matter what the emotion is, it demonstrates the power the narcissist holds in the situation. If you respond calmly and don't take the bait, you can avoid giving them any more power. For example, if your partner says, "the house is a terrible mess, you never do anything around here," you can say, "yes, it could stand to be picked up, should we do that now?" without reacting to the accusation.

It's sometimes better to ignore anything hinted or implied but to respond directly to insults or put-downs by setting a firm boundary. Either way, the key point is to not react in any way that will give the narcissist more of the power he craves.

Remind yourself that he isn't really talking about you in the first place. He's really describing his own inner self—the self that he can't stand to face or deal with. Don't take it personally, but don't let him use it as an excuse to mistreat you. The narcissist's actions may be driven by suffering, but he has no right to inflict suffering on you as his coping strategy.

Codependency often makes it difficult to deal with projection because the codependent person also has a painful relationship with the inner self. You may have received toxic messages in childhood that gave you a distorted sense of who you are. For instance, you may have such a negative self-picture that you find it easy to accept criticism and almost impossible to accept praise.

When someone tells you something good about yourself, you can't hear or it or believe it. When someone tells you something bad about yourself, it feels like the truth.

Your negative self-image comes from your own experiences and has nothing to do with whatever criticism or blame the narcissist is throwing at you. It might feel like he sees the horrible truth about you, but that really isn't what's happening at all. The narcissist cannot see the inner you, for good or bad, so his comments can never represent some special insight into who you really are. No matter what terrible thing he says, he's always describing how he feels about himself. It's always a projection.

It's important to work on your self-esteem, which may mean getting therapy to deal with the toxic beliefs you absorbed in childhood. Whether you're in therapy or not, understanding projection is essential in dealing with narcissistic abuse.

Dealing with Narcissistic Parents

For many people with codependency, the first narcissist they ever met was their mother or father. Establishing boundaries can be much harder with family than with other people because family usually knows you a lot better and has a lot more practice pushing your buttons.

Some people choose not to deal with their parents at all because they can't establish boundaries in any other way. If you still want to maintain a relationship with your parents, learning how to have better boundaries may be the only way to do it.

The key is to detach, which doesn't mean to move far away (although that works for some people) or to stop caring but to stop taking on the responsibility for your parent's feelings. Just because your mother wants something does not mean it is your responsibility to provide it. Just because your father expects you to prioritize him at all times doesn't mean you have to.

For example, if your mother expects you to take her phone calls even when you're busy, you may feel like a bad child if you don't take the call. However, you're not responsible for managing her emotions. Take a step back and detach emotionally, then tell her you'll call her when you're no longer busy. That doesn't make you a bad child—it just means you have to manage your time like everyone else.

Your mother or father may try to guilt-trip you for not going along with what they want. For instance, they may send you texts or leave voice mail messages to blackmail you emotionally. Set clear boundaries when this happens: "If you want me to spend more time with you, I need you to stop sending me this kind of message."

Some people find it easier to establish healthy boundaries when they can keep a little more distance between themselves and their family members. For instance, it might help to stay with friends or at an Airbnb when you're visiting home, rather than to sleep at your parents' house. This allows you to take a little space when you need to withdraw while still spending time with your family.

Ineffective Responses

Some tactics are effective when dealing with a narcissist, and some are ineffective. Remember to avoid these common but ineffective responses, especially if you have a history of codependency:

- Placating the narcissist
- Arguing with the narcissist
- Defending your own actions
- Criticizing the narcissist
- Begging or pleading
- Blaming yourself
- Making empty threats
- Excusing, minimizing, or denying the problem
- Avoiding conflict
- Trying to get the narcissist to understand you

Don't Placate

Placating the narcissist will only backfire because he will interpret your attempts to appease him as a victory. Narcissists see interpersonal conflict in black and white terms—every disagreement has a winner and a loser. If you appease the narcissist, he will only take this as an admission of defeat, encouraging him to continue with the same behaviors. Once you draw a line with a narcissist, you have to stick to that line.

Don't Argue

Arguing back and forth with a narcissist is a lose-lose proposition because it's based on the false assumption that the narcissist shares your desire for eventual agreement and mutual understanding. In reality, the narcissist only cares about who wins and who loses. Facts are irrelevant to the narcissist, so debating things like who said what or who did what can only play into the narcissist's hands. Deflect every attempt to draw you into a debate. The narcissist isn't arguing in good faith anyway, so trying to win an argument or prove your point would only waste your time and energy.

Don't Defend

It's only natural to defend your actions or your motivations when someone is criticizing you, but defending yourself is always a mistake when you're dealing with a narcissist. Why? It's because the narcissist is assuming something that she doesn't have any right to assume, which is that she has the authority to judge your actions as acceptable or unacceptable. The same thing goes for explaining yourself, which tells the narcissist that she has the right to demand explanations. As an independent person, you have the right to make your own decisions. You don't have to defend or explain yourself to anyone.

Don't Criticize

Criticizing the narcissist is a mistake for several different reasons. First, it assumes that the narcissist actually cares about doing the right thing, when in reality, he only cares about getting his own needs met. Second, it opens you up to the narcissist's counterattack—after all, if you can judge him, then he can judge you. Third, it can trigger an explosive burst of narcissistic rage. Narcissists cannot handle even a hint of criticism because it exposes the vulnerability and pain of the inner self. Rather than criticizing the narcissist for his selfish actions, it's better to establish and enforce your own boundaries.

Don't Beg

In the black-and-white mental world of the typical narcissist, those who beg and plead are weak and contemptible, while those who receive these pleas are strong and powerful. When you plead with a narcissist to change his behavior, he sees this as a clear confirmation that he is strong and you are weak. Instead of doing whatever you're begging him to do, the narcissist will simply view you with even more contempt and disregard. It can be hard to remember this, but you are only ever in control of your own actions. Focus on what you can do—not on what he should do.

Don't Blame Yourself

If you cannot control the narcissist's actions (and you really can't), then you cannot be responsible for them either. The only person responsible for any action is the person who commits that action. When the narcissist yells or gets drunk or punches holes in the walls, those actions are his and his alone. It's impossible for you to provoke them or bear any responsibility for them whatsoever. Remember, codependent people have a hard time understanding and establishing boundaries between themselves and others. It may feel like you are somehow to blame for what the narcissist says or does or feels, but you are two separate people and can only be responsible for your own life.

Don't Bluff

Don't ever make a threat you aren't prepared to carry out because the narcissist will take this as a sign that you don't really mean it and that he can ignore any boundaries you try to set. For example, don't say "if I catch you cheating again, I'll move out" unless you fully intend to do exactly that.

Don't Deny It

Denial is one of the strongest instincts the codependent person has, and you'll have to fight against it for a long time if that's part of your history and your personality. When you know something isn't right, it won't help at all to pretend otherwise. It's better to face it and get it dealt with, even if you find that painful or difficult. This includes making excuses for the narcissist's behavior or minimizing how bad the problem really is.

Don't Avoid It

Avoiding a problem is a lot like denying it and will do nothing in the long term to regain your power over your own life. Fleeing the scene of a conversation you have lost control over may sometimes be necessary so you can get your emotions under control and stop playing whatever game the narcissist wants you to play. However, you can't establish boundaries by simply avoiding any conflict, so in the end, you will have to address the situation one way or the other.

Don't Look for Sympathy or Understanding

Trying to get the narcissist to understand where you're coming from or even to sympathize with you is a losing fight. The narcissist isn't interested in understanding other people, only in getting what he needs from them. He may express sympathy under certain conditions, but his ability to actually feel it is limited or nonexistent. The goal in dealing with a narcissist is not to be understood, but to establish boundaries and make sure they're respected.

Dealing with Physical Abuse

Physical abuse is not always the most psychologically damaging form of abuse. Many people find that emotional abuse is more harmful to their overall wellbeing. However, physical abuse is dangerous in a different way because it almost always escalates over time. Many abusers will express intense shame and remorse over their violent acts in the immediate aftermath, but that doesn't mean they won't do it again. They almost certainly will, no matter what they say—and it will almost certainly get worse.

The abuser may try to evade the responsibility for their own violence by blaming it on you, so boundaries are especially important in this type of situation. You can't be responsible for the other person's actions, so if they say you provoked them or drove them to it, they are simply trying to dodge responsibility. It is never your fault.

If your partner is physically abusive, threatening, or violent, it's important not to minimize the problem. Denial can literally be deadly. Seek help immediately and make a plan to ensure your own safety. No matter how strongly you feel about the other person, don't kid yourself about a violent relationship. It's never acceptable for anyone to hit you, and if you don't take steps immediately, it will happen again.

Chapter 7: Next Steps

If you've identified an important relationship in your life as emotionally abusive, the next thing you need to do is to figure out what you want to do about it. Unless your safety is in question, you may not need to decide right away. In fact, you may not be in a good position to decide right away, as your self-esteem may be too badly damaged for you to assess things clearly.

In order to figure out your best course of action, start by setting clear boundaries and rebuilding your damaged self-esteem. Once you've done those things, it should be much easier for you to see whether it makes sense for you to stay in the relationship or not.

We've already explored the concept of setting healthy boundaries, but here are a few more specific examples to help you take this crucial next step in regaining control over your own life.

Boundary Checking

Boundaries can be categorized into one of four types:

- Emotional
- Mental
- Financial
- Physical

Any time you aren't sure whether you have healthy boundaries, run through this list and check each type. To check your emotional boundaries, ask yourself these questions:

- Do I feel responsible for the other person's emotions?
- Do I feel guilty when I don't do what they want me to do?
- Do I find myself giving unsolicited advice?
- Do I find myself blaming the other person?
- Do I accept blame from the other person?

If you answered "yes" to any of these questions, you need to work on having healthier emotional boundaries.

To check your mental boundaries, ask yourself these questions:

- Have my opinions changed to match the other person's?
- Do I feel uncertain about what my opinions really are?
- Do I get defensive or angry when we disagree?
- Am I easily influenced?

If you answered "yes" to any of these questions, you need to work on having healthier mental boundaries.

To check your financial boundaries, ask yourself these questions:

- Do I give the other person money when I can't really afford to or don't really want to?
- Do I loan them things when I don't really want to?
- Do I pay for meals or housing when I don't really want to?
- Have I given the other person access to my bank account or credit card when I would rather have said no?

If you answered "yes" to any of these questions, you need to work on having healthier financial boundaries.

To check your physical boundaries, ask yourself these questions:

- Do I let the other person into my physical space when I don't feel comfortable with it?
- Do I spend time with the other person when I want or need to be doing something else?
- Does the other person violate my privacy in any way?
- Do I agree to sexual contact when I don't really want it?

If you answered "yes" to any of these questions, you need to work on having healthier physical boundaries.

There's more than one way to categorize boundaries, and some situations won't fit easily into one of these four categories. Boundary checking can help you learn how to recognize situations where you need to establish a healthier boundary, even if they don't seem to be easy to categorize.

Rebuilding Your Self-Esteem

As you begin the work of establishing healthy boundaries, you should also take whatever steps are needed to rebuild your self-esteem. That will help give you the clarity you need to make the best decision for your future.

Here are a few simple things you can do to heal some of the damage to your self-esteem.

Take Care of Yourself: taking better care of yourself will boost your self-esteem and will also help you feel like you deserve to be happy. Start with anything you might have been neglecting, such as personal hygiene or wearing outfits that make you feel good about yourself. Make a point of looking sharp (whatever that means to you) on a daily basis. Get enough sleep every night and incorporate exercise into your daily routine. Eat healthy food, and take the time to really enjoy your meals. Clean your home and keep it tidy. Any little thing you can do to improve your own mental and emotional state, go ahead and do it. You'll start to feel better about yourself and become less vulnerable to criticism.

Challenge Negative Thought Patterns: your instincts will tell you that your negative thoughts are accurate, but they are actually distorted thought patterns you've picked up along the way. Challenge your negative thoughts by learning to spot them, and consciously counteract them with more positive assessments. Make a list of everything you like about yourself and remind yourself of something from the list every time a negative thought goes through your head. If you can't come up with enough items to make a list, that's because your self-esteem is badly damaged and not because you don't have any positive qualities. Ask a trusted friend to help you make your list. Use it even if you don't agree with it yet. For instance, if you find yourself thinking, "I am ugly," remind yourself that your friend thinks you have a lovely smile.

Set Positive Goals: positive goals should always be realistic rather than grandiose. Completing an eight-week cooking course would be a realistic goal, while becoming a celebrity chef might be more of a daydream for most people. Don't set yourself up for failure by setting a farfetched goal. Instead, use realistic positive goals to keep you motivated. Every time you hit a new milestone, you'll feel great about it—and you can always set a new milestone a little further down the road. Making a to-do list can be especially helpful because you'll get a little boost to your confidence and self-esteem every time you cross an item off the list.

Take up a Hobby: pursue something you've always wanted to do or take up a new interest. Learn how to play chess or paint or craft. Do something for your own sake that will make you feel happy, without worrying about whether anyone else would approve or not. When you're just getting started, you might want to avoid sharing your new interest with anyone who might be critical. Your new hobby is for you, and until you have strong enough emotional boundaries to take criticism in stride, it might be a good idea to avoid leaving yourself vulnerable to outside opinions.

Should I Stay, or Should I Go?

Once you've done your best to establish clearer boundaries and build up your self-esteem, it's time to take a good, close look at your relationship and decide what you want to do next.

Researchers have developed a few different models to describe how people make the decision to stay in a relationship or leave it. These models don't necessarily describe how people *should* make this important decision, only how they actually *do* decide. Still, knowing how other people go about the process can help you get started.

One of these models is called "interdependence theory." According to this theory, people decide what to do based on a fairly simple comparison of costs and benefits. No relationship is perfect, so people decide to stay in a relationship when the benefits seem to be more significant than the costs, and they decide to leave the relationship when the costs seem to be more significant than the benefits.

People most often do this without consciously thinking about it, but some people do sit down and write out a list of pluses and minuses. This can be helpful, because you may find that one side of the list is a lot weightier than the other once you sit down and write it out.

However, some researchers think that interdependence theory is too simplistic. People often stay in relationships in which the negatives outweigh the positives, and interdependence theory cannot account for that. For one thing, people know that normal relationships go through ups and downs, so they don't want to bail out immediately when things seem more negative than positive.

The "investment model" was created to fill in some of the gaps interdependence theory doesn't cover. According to the investment model, people usually weigh three different factors when they're trying to decide whether to stay in a relationship or not.

The first factor is "relationship satisfaction," which is the simple cost-benefit comparison described by interdependence theory. If the positives outweigh the negatives, you have good relationship satisfaction.

The second factor is "investment," meaning how much you have invested in the relationship. This includes the amount of time you've been together, your happy or otherwise significant memories together, your shared friends, your shared wealth property, and any children you may have together. The more you have invested, the more reluctant you'll be to leave.

The third factor is "alternatives," meaning that most people are quick to leave a relationship if they think they can do better but are more reluctant to leave if they think they can't.

The investment model covers the complexities better than interdependence theory and can give you some additional tools for making your decision. However, it also illustrates how important it is to work on your boundaries and self-esteem. If your self-esteem is very low, you might not feel like you could do better than your current relationship when you really could. If your self-esteem is healthy and your self-confidence is high, you might conclude that you don't really need to be with anyone anyway. Is it really worse to be single than to be in an unhappy and abusive relationship?

Some people will stay in a relationship even when the costs clearly outweigh any benefits, when their unhappiness outweighs any investment they may have made, and when they could either do better with someone else or on their own. Neither interdependence theory nor the investment model can explain why people do that, as it can only make them unhappy not to leave the relationship at that point.

According to recent research, the most common reason for staying in an unhappy relationship is the fear of hurting the other person, combined with a general tendency to put the other person's needs first. As you know, codependent people have a strong tendency to do exactly that. Unfortunately for the codependent person, the narcissist does not share this self-sacrificing tendency. While many narcissists don't like to be alone, they will leave a relationship without a second thought if they can get their need for narcissistic supply met by someone else.

If you're codependent, you should take a hard look at the relationship in its entirety and especially at the person you're in the relationship with—if you have so much invested in your history with this person that you don't want to cut them out of your life completely (for instance, if the narcissist in question is your parent or sibling), then you'll need to set firm boundaries to make things work. If the narcissist in your life is your romantic partner, you can't expect things to get better or to go back to the way they used to be when things were happy between you. The narcissist might love-bomb you for a little while just to keep you from leaving but will never give you consistent love and respect.

As someone with a history of codependency, you may feel deeply responsible for their wellbeing and happiness. You may genuinely believe that they won't be okay without you. However, you cannot count on them to show you the same level of loyalty or concern. If they meet someone new, they will probably leave. Is it really worth it to be unhappy when the person you're sacrificing so much for will not reciprocate?

Some difficult relationships can be saved with couple's therapy, and if your partner is willing to go to counseling with you, then that's a positive sign. Some relationships can't be saved, and some should not be saved.

People often know they should leave a relationship a long time before they actually leave. Why is it so hard to end an emotionally abusive relationship? Often, the answer is trauma bonding.

When you are abused or mistreated, the emotional pain and humiliation of the experience do contrast sharply with your happy memories of the good times you previously shared together. This sets you up to get stuck because you're so desperate for those good feelings to return that any kindness or warmth from the other person can produce intense feelings of togetherness and affection. This is trauma bonding, and it's the same process as "Stockholm Syndrome," where hostages become emotionally attached to their own kidnappers.

Trauma bonding can make the idea of leaving the relationship even more upsetting because you have become emotionally dependent on the abuser's occasional acts of warmth and affection. Unfortunately, kindness is an exception, and the ongoing pattern of abuse is the rule.

If you decide to leave, you'll need a plan.

Leaving an Abusive Relationship

If your relationship is not worth saving, the next step is to leave in a way that keeps you safe and secure. Here are some steps you can take to help you move on:

- Take steps to rebuild your self-esteem by taking care of yourself, challenging negative thought patterns, and setting positive goals.

- Take steps to rebuild your independence by taking up new interests and hobbies and building friendships outside the relationship.
- Build an emotional support network by going to therapy or joining a group for codependents or other people in a similar situation.
- Talk to your doctor or other healthcare professional about the abuse.
- Call the National Domestic Violence Hotline at 1-800-799-7233 or 1-800-787-3224 for trained assistance on how to safely leave. They can direct you to a free domestic violence shelter if needed.
- Reconnect with supportive and nonjudgmental friends and family members.
- Practice setting boundaries and being assertive.
- Make a list of the abuser's usual tactics so that he won't be able to push your buttons. Mentally rehearse your responses.
- Set aside money or arrange a place to stay so you won't be dependent on the relationship for your own survival.
- Set up a safe place to go when you leave, preferably one unknown to your partner.

- Talk to a friend and arrange a code word to mean that you are in danger or need to be picked up.
- Get a prepaid cell phone and leave it someplace where it won't be found, so you can call for help if you need it without your partner knowing.
- Commit any phone numbers you might need to memory.
- Make copies of any important personal documents and keep them someplace other than the home.
- Set aside clothing, money, food, and any necessary medications.
- If you're married or have children with your partner, get a lawyer to make sure your rights are protected before the process starts.
- Have a safety plan in place if there is any question or the possibility of physical violence.
- Once you actually leave, cut off all contact completely so the abuser can't drag you back in with manipulation tactics.
- If you can't cut off contact for some reason, keep the contact to the bare minimum and don't let the abuser draw you into any extended conversations.

Remember, the narcissistic abuser will interpret your decision to end the relationship as a personal attack and a defeat. His fragile ego will not allow him to accept your decision easily, and he may use any number of manipulative strategies to remain in your life somehow. This can include begging and pleading, promising to treat you better, threatening to hurt himself, threatening to hurt you, spreading hurtful stories or lies about you, showing up in places where he thinks you might be and trying to communicate with you through other people.

Be prepared ahead of time for him to do whatever it takes to keep you connected to him, even if that just means trying to get an emotional reaction out of you on social media. No matter what he does, it's just a power game—don't let him pull you back in once you've made your decision.

Toxic Family Relationships

When the abusive narcissist in your life is a family member rather than a romantic partner, it can sometimes be even harder to set healthy boundaries or end the relationship if needed. You may realize that a parent or sibling is narcissistic but still want to maintain the family relationship on some level. In this situation, the healthiest thing you can do for the relationship is often to establish firm boundaries and get some distance.

For instance, you may decide that the only relationship you can handle with your mother is to have coffee in a public place once a month. You may decide that you can handle visiting your father once or twice a year, but only if you stay in a hotel and keep all conversations on "safe" topics. Whatever boundary you set is up to you, but you will need to work on maintaining that boundary if you want the relationship to function in a healthy way.

Some people do succeed in having healthier relationships with toxic family members by establishing firm boundaries and sticking to them. If you just can't do that, or if the relationship is too destructive for you even to consider it, then the same basic process applies as with an abusive partner. Once you make the decision to stop engaging with an abusive family member, don't let them manipulate you into keeping the connection open or responding to their manipulative tactics.

Remember that other family members may handle the same situation differently and avoid judging them for doing things as they think best. Your sister might not be ready to cut her off her relationship with your abusive parents, or she might have her own way of setting boundaries that work for her. Either way, don't ask her to pick sides. If your relationship with her is healthy, then you can both respect each other's choices.

Chapter 8: Long-Term Effects of Narcissistic Abuse

Narcissistic abuse has many long-term effects, including an increased tendency toward either narcissism or codependency. If you experienced long-term narcissistic abuse in childhood, you might suffer from some or all of the following symptoms.

Insecure Attachment: Children with healthy and happy family relationships develop the ability to form secure attachments—meaning that they are able to connect emotionally with others while still maintaining healthy boundaries. Usually, children who experience abuse or neglect develop an insecure attachment style, which can take the form or either anxiety or avoidance. If you tend to chase after loving relationships with others, your attachment style is anxious. If you tend to protect yourself by refusing or avoiding intimate relationships, your attachment style is avoidant. Some people have an anxious attachment style in some situations and an avoidant attachment style in others.

Neediness: Intense neediness is a symptom of insecure

attachment. This kind of neediness is often episodic, meaning that you may give other people the impression of being independent and not needing much from others until you get overwhelmed, at which point you become extremely needy toward friends and family members. This is basically a panic reaction driven by a deep belief that your most basic emotional needs will not be met.

Self-Criticism: When children don't get the love, attention, and emotional support they need from their parents, they often respond by blaming themselves. They focus on fixing whatever they're doing wrong so their parents will love them, not realizing that the narcissistic parent is incapable of giving them what they need. This tendency to self-criticize carries over into adulthood, making them vulnerable to narcissistic abuse. Because they crave validation and affection, they are vulnerable to love-bombing. When the narcissist stops idealizing them and begins devaluing them, they are primed to believe it.

Shrinking: Narcissistic parents cannot handle the normal emotional needs of their children and may react with dramatic displays of anger or self-pity whenever the child expresses any needs at all. Children often respond to this by shrinking up, a tendency that can easily carry over into adult life. Do you find yourself trying to take up as little space as possible when interacting with others? Do you find yourself putting other people at the center while you stay in the shadows? Do you feel selfish whenever you express your needs? If so, you may have learned this behavior in childhood due to narcissistic parenting.

Sensitivity: Victims of long-term narcissistic abuse often think of themselves as empathetic, or highly attuned to the emotions of others. While this is often the case, the reason for it is the abuse they experienced. When you always have to walk on eggshells to avoid upsetting a narcissistic parent, you can become extraordinarily sensitive to the tiniest hint of another person's emotional state. Rather than simply being an indication of how kind and caring you are, unusual sensitivity can be a sign of how much abuse you have suffered. Some researchers believe that the main reason some abused children become narcissistic while others become codependent is simply that some people are more aggressive than others. Abused children who are more aggressive are more likely to deal with the abuse by becoming narcissistic, while those who are less aggressive are more likely to deal with it by becoming more empathetic (and ultimately codependent).

Although both narcissism and codependency are common reactions to childhood abuse, abused children are also more likely to develop other long-term problems. Increased rates of eating disorders, substance abuse, obesity, heart disease, and mental health problems, in general, have all been linked to emotional abuse in childhood.

Emotional abuse in childhood can also lead to other symptoms such as regression to an earlier stage of emotional development.

Effects of Abuse

Even if you don't believe you ever experienced narcissistic abuse as a child, experiencing abuse as an adult can still cause a number of surprising symptoms.

When most people hear the word "abuse," they immediately think of violence. Narcissistic abuse isn't always violent, but the damage it causes can be just as profound. The short-term effects of emotional abuse can include:

- Feelings of shame, confusion, fear, and powerlessness
- Unexplained aches and pains
- Mood swings
- Elevated heart rate
- Upsetting dreams
- Inability to concentrate

You may have experienced some or all of these symptoms without even recognizing them as the effects of emotional abuse. The brain and the rest of the body are closely connected, so stress hormones in the brain can cause a range of other symptoms.

The long-term symptoms of emotional abuse are similar to the short-term symptoms, and can include:

- Unexplained chronic pain
- Anxiety problems
- Sleep disorders, such as insomnia
- Social isolation
- Lingering feelings of guilt and shame

These are all common effects of emotional abuse and may indicate that you are suffering from something called narcissistic victim syndrome.

Narcissist Victim Syndrome

Even after you succeed in leaving an emotionally abusive relationship, you may suffer from confusing and painful symptoms. For example, you may have nightmares about the abuse you experienced. You may have flashbacks wherein you relive a traumatic incident. You may find yourself having intense reactions (both physical and emotional) to anything that reminds you of the abuse.

You may find it hard to keep negative thoughts or memories out of your mind, including negative thoughts about yourself and your life. You might feel guilty or ashamed about what happened. You might feel disconnected from other people or unable to relate to them. You might have problems with insomnia, or trouble concentrating. Finally, you might have symptoms of hypervigilance, including being startled easily or constantly feeling like you have to watch out for potential threats.

These are all symptoms of narcissistic abuse syndrome or narcissist victim syndrome. This syndrome is not yet an official mental health diagnosis, but the symptoms have been observed by therapists who specialize in helping the victims of narcissistic abuse.

Narcissistic victim syndrome doesn't happen by accident. Emotional abusers intentionally disorient and confuse their victims to exercise power over them and destroy their ability to see the situation for what it is. Even after the victim leaves the situation and escapes the abuser, the sense of confusion and disorientation can linger for a long time. That's because the symptoms are not just emotional reactions, but the result of changes to the brain of the victim.

Effects on the Brain

Many of the symptoms of narcissistic victim syndrome are caused by damage to two important areas of the brain: the hippocampus and the amygdala, both of which are affected by the stress hormone cortisol.

The hippocampus is the section of the brain's temporal lobes responsible for storing short-term memories so they can be converted into long-term memories.

Unfortunately, cortisol causes the hippocampus to shrink. Abuse and manipulation flood the brain with cortisol, damaging the hippocampus, and reducing the victim's ability to form neural pathways. This does damage the victim's ability to think clearly or make important changes, such as leaving the abuser or building a new life.

While it shrinks the hippocampus, cortisol grows another section of the brain called the amygdala. The amygdala is responsible for the most basic and primal emotions, such as fear and rage. An overstimulated amygdala causes symptoms such as hypervigilance and panic attacks.

Damage to the hippocampus appears to be cumulative, meaning that the longer you are exposed to the abuse, the higher your cortisol levels will go and the more your hippocampus will shrink.

As your hippocampus shrinks and your amygdala grows, you find yourself increasingly responding with the most primal and instinctive reactions—the "fight or flight" responses of the amygdala. Fight or flight is a basic instinctive reaction to an immediate threat, such as a dangerous animal. The experience of being abused is essentially the same (as far as the brain is concerned) as being constantly in the presence of a growling attack dog.

The combination of a weakened hippocampus and a strengthened amygdala can leave the victim disoriented, foggy, and prone to intense anxiety, especially when confronted by any reminders of the abuse. These are the main symptoms of narcissistic victim syndrome.

Post-Traumatic Stress Disorder

Narcissistic victim syndrome has similar symptoms to PTSD or post-traumatic stress disorder, which can also be caused by some types of abuse.

PTSD is often triggered by experiencing a deeply upsetting or frightening event, such as seeing an act of extreme violence or cruelty. The symptoms of PTSD include flashbacks, nightmares, insomnia, hypervigilance, intrusive thoughts, and sudden outbursts of anger, much like narcissistic victim syndrome.

PTSD can be caused by a single traumatic incident—for example, a soldier may suffer from PTSD after seeing a friend killed in combat. When the trauma is caused by an ongoing series of incidents, a therapist is more likely to diagnose "complex post-traumatic stress disorder," which can have more severe and long-lasting symptoms than regular PTSD.

Both PTSD and complex PTSD can cause additional long-term symptoms. Sufferers may lose faith in whatever belief system they previously accepted, such as the religion they were raised in. They may develop a negative view of the world as a fundamentally hostile and dangerous place, of other people in general as dangerous and untrustworthy, or of the self as unworthy.

They may lose the ability to regulate their own emotions, leading to violent mood swings, including sorrow, anger, or suicidal thoughts. They may become dissociative, not seeming to react emotionally to the trauma they experienced. In some cases, they may not even be able to remember what happened. They may be obsessed with the person who was responsible for their abuse, or with the relationship itself. They may have difficulty in maintaining healthy relationships or a tendency to get involved in toxic relationships. They may also be at increased risk for substance abuse, addiction problems, and self-harming behaviors.

After reading this description, you may find it hard to tell the difference between narcissistic victim syndrome and complex post-traumatic stress disorder. The two have similar symptoms and can both be caused by narcissistic abuse.

It is not necessarily important to know which diagnosis better explains your symptoms unless you are in therapy and getting professional treatment for the effects of abuse. Only a therapist can give you a diagnosis, and your own therapist will always be in a better position to make an accurate diagnosis than anyone else.

The most important point at the moment is simply to understand that narcissistic abuse can have long-term effects and that you are not alone in experiencing these effects. If you've been having trouble with insomnia, intrusive thoughts, difficulty concentrating, or any of the other symptoms described in this chapter, then the abuse you experienced might very well be the reason.

The good news is that your situation is far from hopeless. Even though long-term abuse affects the brain in negative ways, this damage can be reversed and eventually healed. If you suspect that you are suffering from the physical and emotional effects of narcissistic abuse, seek out professional help from a qualified counselor.

Self-Isolation After Narcissistic Abuse

Abusers often seek to isolate their victims, to prevent them from seeking help or making the decision to leave the relationship. To an abusive narcissist, the idea that you might give some of your time and attention to anyone other than him is simply intolerable.

A narcissistic abuser will use all kinds of strategies to pull you away from the other people in your life. He may try to convince you not to trust them, or he may simply interfere with the relationship in petty little ways. It's easy to become disconnected from friends and family, but it is sometimes much harder to reconnect with them after the damage is done.

When you leave the relationship, it would only be natural for you to renew those connections—but this doesn't always happen right away. In many cases, the victim of abuse continues to be isolated, sometimes for years after the abusive relationship has ended.

This can happen for many reasons. Depression and anxiety can both be triggered by abuse, and people tend to become more isolated when they're depressed and anxious. Depression can sap your motivation to do anything at all, and anxiety can make social contact too intimidating to contemplate.

On top of that, the intense self-criticism and hypervigilance of the abuse victim can both make it difficult to renew old social connections or establish new ones. Hypervigilance tells you that other people are out to hurt you and cannot be trusted. Self-criticism makes you feel like no one would want to spend time with you anyway.

The mental fog and confusion of narcissistic victim syndrome can also make it difficult for you to focus on the outside world—days, weeks, and months can seem to slip away from you so that even if you have a vague plan of reconnecting with others socially, you just don't get around to it.

You may also find that you have no idea what your own interests are and you don't even know what social activities you might enjoy. This could be especially disorienting if you used to have hobbies, passions, and social activities of your own. It can feel like you no longer know yourself, and in a way, this may be true. Abusers often gave that effect on their victims.

One way to understand the process of narcissistic abuse is to think of it as a deliberate attempt to gain complete ownership of another person. The narcissist systematically destroys his victim's sense of self so that he can control them even in their own inner thoughts. That's at least part of the reason for the put-downs, the mind games, and especially the gaslighting. Nothing gives the abuser more power than for the victim to lose faith in his own ability to tell what's real and what isn't.

Disoriented and confused by the abuser's games, the victim often tries to make sense of the situation by accepting the narcissist's own views of the situation. For example, the victim may become convinced that she is responsible for the abuse, that the relationship isn't abusive in the first place, that other people are untrustworthy or harmful, and that the abuser is the only person who loves or understands her.

The victim of narcissistic abuse can eventually become so thoroughly brainwashed by the abuser that she can no longer remember who she really is, or she can no longer connect with any thoughts and feelings that are authentically her own. It's as if the victim's self has been erased and replaced with the narcissist's self-serving projections. Because the core of the narcissist's true self is intense self-loathing, the victim often internalizes all the shame and pain the narcissist feels toward himself.

Even after taking the huge step of separating yourself from the person who abused you, you might not be able to reconnect to your own sense of self right away. Without a clear idea of who you are and what you want to do, it's hard to make plans with anyone else. For many abuse victims, it can seem easier just to stay isolated, effectively compounding the damage originally caused by the abuser.

To overcome this tendency to self-isolate, you need to rebuild your sense of self. Reconnecting with friends and family members can help you remember who you are and can go a long way to rebuilding your emotional support networks—especially if you reconnect with people whom you had a healthy relationship with in the first place. You may worry that they won't want to reconnect with you after all this time, but most of them will probably understand what happened and be happy to hear from you.

It can also be helpful to reconnect with your past in other ways. Some people find it useful to think back on what they used to enjoy before the abusive relationship even started. For example, if you used to go out for karaoke, it might be fun to try it again and see if you still enjoy it—especially if you can reconnect with your old karaoke buddies.

Some people find that so much time has passed, and their lives have changed so much that they no longer identify with whoever they used to be and whatever they used to enjoy doing. If that's the case for you, it might be more effective to find a new interest by trying out different hobbies. You can pick things almost at random from an adult education catalog, trying new things until you find one you really take an interest in. Painting, Tai Chi, Yoga, or a new language—almost anything that gets you out of the house and around some new people can be a positive course of action. By discovering what you enjoy and making new friends, you can begin rebuilding your damaged sense of self.

As you work on reconnecting or building new connections with other people, don't forget to work on healing your sense of self-esteem and especially your ability to like yourself. Paradoxically, people are more likely to become isolated from others when they don't like themselves much and find it painful to be alone. People are more likely to enjoy happy and healthy relationships with others when they enjoy their own company and can handle being alone without discomfort.

You may not feel capable of liking yourself right away, but you can improve your self-esteem by acting as if you do. As discussed previously in the chapter on how to respond to narcissistic abuse, simple steps like dressing nicely or wearing makeup can help you feel better about yourself. Even something as simple as cleaning your house can help you start to feel a little bit better—for the simple reason that you are taking care of yourself again.

Chapter 9: Recovering from Narcissistic Abuse

Although narcissistic abuse does have long-term effects, that doesn't mean that you will never be able to overcome those effects. The psychological and emotional wounds of narcissistic abuse will heal with time—as long as you give them the chance to do so. Even the effects of abuse on your brain can be reversed as you recover. Like a broken bone growing back stronger than before, you may even find that your new self is healthier and more resilient than the person you were before you suffered the abuse.

Waking Up

The first stage in healing is to understand how narcissistic personality disorder develops and what narcissism really means. Once you understand and accept this, a lot of things that seemed complicated and confusing should make a lot more sense. For example, you may have wondered how your partner could be so kind, loving, and attentive in some situations and so unpredictable, cruel, and undermining others. Now that you have a clearer understanding of narcissistic abuse, you know that there is really no contradiction at all. Both behaviors were merely expressions of your partner's underlying narcissism, which drives him to interact with others in a pattern that is much more predictable than you may have realized:

1- Idealization: in this phase, the narcissist projects all his fantasies about ideal love and support onto the new person in his life, giving them the false impression that he can heal their wounds and securing a new source of narcissistic supply.
2- Devaluation: in this phase, the narcissist projects all his inner fears, self-hatred, and insecurities onto the other person, destroying their sense of self. He may return to the idealization phase temporarily to keep his victim hooked but will always come back to the devaluation phase in a little while.
3- Discarding: in this phase, the narcissist finds someone else to provide him with narcissistic supply and discards the previous victim, often without warning.

Not many people will leave the narcissist in the idealization phase—it simply feels too good, especially for someone with unresolved childhood wounds. Generally speaking, only experts at spotting narcissists will recognize this stage for what it is and escape in time.

Many people will only leave once they are well into the devaluation phase and have already suffered a lot of damage. Many don't leave even then and are blind-sided when the narcissist leaves them for someone else. Either way, the first stage of healing is waking up: recognizing the narcissist for what he really is.

Highly empathic people are potentially vulnerable to narcissists for several reasons. One reason is that the childhood experiences that produce codependency also tend to produce children highly attentive to the emotions of the people around them. Another reason is the nature of empathy itself. If you're always the one who can see the other side of the story, if you're willing to meet people halfway, if you always want to understand and forgive, then you will find it much harder to face the harsh truth about the narcissist.

The narcissist's expressions of love might be convincing, but he is always in love with his own reflection. His remorse might seem genuine, but he is fundamentally incapable of loving other people in a healthy and mutually supportive way. His suffering is real, but his method of dealing with this suffering is to drain other people and then throw them away.

The gift of your empathy and understanding is wasted on the narcissist, who will only use it to keep you hooked while he systematically drains you of your sense of self. The sooner you start to think of the narcissist as a type of vampire, the sooner you will take the next step in the healing process: stepping out into the sunlight, where vampires cannot go.

Breaking Contact

Ending your relationship with the narcissist is an important step, but it will be hard to maintain unless you go all the way. Completely breaking contact is essential for healing because otherwise, the narcissist will do everything within his power to maintain control.

For example, if you move out of your abuser's house but stay in contact by phone, he will still have the ability to use almost every tactic in his manipulative repertoire. Even if you're determined not to go back to him, he can get a power thrill just by saying something he knows will push your buttons. The same is true if you remain in contact by email or if he keeps sending you messages through friends or family members. He may try to win you back with empty promises, or he may just try to hurt you or make you mad.

If you want to start healing as soon as possible, it's essential to break contact with the narcissist completely. Refuse to see him. Don't answer his phone calls. Delete his emails without reading them. Block his texts. Tell friends and family members who are still in contact with him that you aren't interested in getting any messages.

Along with breaking off all contact, resist the urge to check up on him or see how he's doing. Even glancing at his social media pages would be a mistake. One of the things he's most likely to do is to post pictures of himself having a great time with someone else to make you jealous, or ranting about how much you've mistreated him, or anything else he thinks might trigger an emotional reaction.

It's not easy to do this, but your goal should be not only to cut off all contact with the narcissistic abuser but to remove every last thread connecting their life to yours—including your thoughts.

If you do happen to run into the narcissist at a family event or in a public place, you can use something called the "gray rock" technique to keep them from regaining any of the power they used to have over you. As the name implies, the idea in this technique is to be like a wall of granite—flat and emotionless, not reacting to anything.

If you have children with a narcissist, you may not have any choice except to remain in contact with them. In this situation, the narcissist will probably try to retain as much emotional power over you as possible, perhaps for years.

To defend yourself from continued abuse in this situation, limit your contact to the bare minimum required by the court-ordered custody agreement. These agreements often allow you to specify the type and frequency of contact. For instance, you may be able to require your co-parent to call the children only at scheduled times or to refrain from contacting you except by email.

Some family courts can appoint a Guardian ad Litem to safeguard the legal interests of your children, or a Parent Coordinator to handle scheduling issues and any necessary communication.

Whatever the specific arrangements, make sure your custody agreement spells everything out in as much detail as possible and leaves no room for ambiguity.

Resist the urge to ask your children about your former partner, and never ask your children to carry messages for you. Even if it isn't easy to break off all contact, you need to get as close as possible to no-contact in order to heal.

Understanding What Happened

Once you have some distance, the next step in the recovery process is to understand what really happened.

To understand what happened means to face the truth. Even after leaving an abusive relationship, you may still feel deeply conflicted and confused about the abuser and your relationship. You may still feel powerfully drawn toward them and the intense emotions they bring up in you. You may still feel sympathy for them and the things they've suffered in life, especially if you feel that these things explain their abusive behavior. You may still want to believe that they really loved you and that the toxic and destructive things they did were not the whole story of your relationship.

If you want to heal, it's crucial for you to accept the fact that they hurt you on purpose. The narcissist is not an innocent victim or a confused person in need of sympathy, but a willfully manipulative and destructive individual who caused you tremendous harm for purely selfish reasons. As long as you continue to give him the benefit of the doubt, the narcissist will continue to be able to hurt you.

Once you've accepted this truth, the next step in healing is to admit something you may not be comfortable admitting—that you've known the truth for a long time. This isn't easy to admit, because it's painful to think of how much trouble you could have saved yourself if you had only paid attention to the red flags the first time you saw them.

As hard as it may be, you need to think back over your history with the narcissist and remember the warning signs, because they will help keep you safe in future relationships.

When you were still in the idealization phase, and the narcissist was love bombing you, did a little voice in your head tell you it all sounded too good to be true?

Did you notice the narcissist pushing your boundaries or trying to get you to commit too quickly? Did you notice him testing for your reactions, saying or doing things that weren't quite appropriate? Did you catch him in a lie, or suspect that his stories were a little grandiose?

Whatever your moment may have been, there was almost certainly at least one, and there may have been several. Over time and as things got worse, there were probably many such moments—times when you knew something was really wrong but denied it or rationalized it or made excuses for your abuser.

It will almost certainly be painful to admit this to yourself, but once you admit it, you can move on. There's no need to blame yourself or feel ashamed for not leaving sooner.

You were vulnerable to the narcissist's power games, and he took advantage.

The next stage in the process is to ask yourself why. What was it that made you vulnerable?

Do you have a deep need for security, perhaps as a result of being neglected as a child?

Do you have a need for displays of love, perhaps because you never got the love and affection you needed when you were young?

Do you have a need for praise and validation or a pervasive sense of not being good enough?

Whatever your wounds are and whatever you need from other people, these are the vulnerabilities the narcissist exploited.

Healing

Rebuilding your damaged self-esteem is a long process and includes everything we've discussed in previous chapters from basic self-care to developing new hobbies and interests. However, you shouldn't limit your goals to just getting back to how you were before this abusive relationship happened. If you weren't already wounded and vulnerable in some way, the abuser would never have been able to take advantage of you. To break free of the abuse and ensure that it never happens to you again, you must heal the wounds that made you vulnerable in the first place.

Some people find it helpful to visualize their "inner child," the self that suffered some childhood trauma. For example, if you were raised by a narcissistic parent who treated you without warmth or empathy, your inner child may be in need of warmth and empathy. If you were never praised but always criticized, your inner child may be in need of praise and acceptance. If you felt abandoned, your inner child may have a need for security.

Whatever it is, you can heal your inner child by giving her what she needed and never had. You can take your urge to care for others and refocus it on your inner child, directing all your warmth and empathy toward her instead of the narcissist. You can give her the praise you always wanted to hear and the acceptance you always wanted to feel. By creating a new life for yourself without manipulation or abuse, you can give your inner child the sense of security she always craved.

There's a lot more to the concept of the inner child than we have space for here, but you can find numerous self-help programs dedicated to this theme online. The idea of the inner child is also explored in many different self-help books and is a central theme in some types of therapy. If this idea seems useful to you, there are plenty of resources available to get you started.

Another healing method some people find effective is to express what happened to them in some way. This could be as simple as keeping a daily journal to record your feelings, or it could even be some form of artistic expression such as poetry, songwriting, dance, or fiction. The idea is to take what's inside you and give it a chance to get out, so you don't have to carry it around with you anymore.

Expressing your feelings can help you reconnect with them, especially if the abuse has left you feeling alienated from your own emotions. It can help you restore your inner self and may teach you many things about what you just experienced that you were not previously aware of.

Many people also find it deeply healing to volunteer. Helping others in some way will get you out of the house and counteract the tendency to self-isolate after narcissistic abuse. It will get you interacting with other people and having a positive impact on their daily lives. This can also do a lot to counteract the damage to your self-esteem. When you help other people, the negative things the abuser wanted you to believe about yourself will start to lose their hold on you.

The changes to your brain caused by narcissistic abuse can also be reversed or mitigated in various ways. For example, studies have shown that Eye Movement Desensitization and Reprocessing therapy can actually regrow a damaged hippocampus while preventing the amygdala from becoming overstimulated. Emotional Freedom Technique, another form of therapy, has also been shown to help with chronic anxiety.

Aromatherapy, the use of essential oils, and the practice of mindfulness meditation have all been shown to benefit the amygdala and the hippocampus, reversing the damage caused by narcissistic abuse.

Starting Over

As you go through the steps of healing, it's important to remember that no one heals in a linear fashion. You can't just go through a stage and then leave it behind, secure in the knowledge that those feelings will never come back again. That isn't reality and will leave you unprepared unemotionally for the ups and downs of the real healing process.

You should expect to backslide every now and then. You'll feel confident and independent for a while, then suddenly fall apart and start missing the person who abused you or finding yourself tormented by intrusive thoughts again. This is totally normal, and the best thing you can do for yourself when it happens is simply to remember that. Although we heal in stages, there's no rule that says the stages always move forward and never slide back.

Despite this fact, if you keep working on healing and taking the steps you need to take, you will eventually find yourself at the last stage in the healing process—the stage in which you are ready to stop focusing on what happened and start focusing on what you want to do with your life.

After you have woken up to the reality of narcissistic abuse, broken contact with the abuser, have taken steps to understand what happened, and have worked on healing your inner wounds, the final stage in the healing process is to move forward with your own life as a free person. If you've done the work to heal from the abuse you suffered, you may even find that you are stronger and more resilient now than you have ever been before.

Of course, your new life actually started the moment you decided to begin the process of leaving the abuser and healing the effects of the abuse. Still, the earlier stages were more focused on the past—you accepted the facts about what the abuser did, then focused on healing the trauma and loss of past events. These steps were important, but it's also important to know when to move on from the past and reorient yourself toward the future.

Think of the earlier stages as being something like a cocoon, in which you turned inward and focused on making the changes you needed to make. Now it's time to leave the cocoon behind and fly off into your new life.

As you do so, you can have the confidence of knowing that you are much better prepared to recognize and defend yourself against narcissists than you were before. You know how they operate, you know your own vulnerabilities, and you've done everything in your power to heal those vulnerabilities.

You have every reason to be confident. Even so, there is more than one type of narcissist, and you may still be more vulnerable than you realize—especially to someone who seems capable of healing your wounds from the abusive relationship you so recently got out of.

If you meet someone new and they seem appealing, you need to know how to tell who you're dealing with. You need to develop the skills to spot narcissists early, to keep narcissists and other potential abusers from spotting any vulnerabilities you may still have, and to draw firm boundaries early on when there is any question. Once you develop these skills, you don't need to be scared about meeting new people.

Forewarned is forearmed as the saying goes. Knowing that you have the necessary skillset to keep yourself safe should help give you the confidence you need to enjoy your new life and everything it has to offer.

Chapter 10: 7 Tips to Avoid Toxic Relationships

If you want to be safe from narcissistic abuse, then closing yourself off to others is *not* the way to do it. Why? It is because living in a state of constant fear and paranoia is a dead giveaway to the potential abuser, letting him know that you have an abuse history.

All he has to do to win your trust is position himself in just the right way, convincing you that he is the one who can heal your wounds, the one who will treat you the way you deserve to be treated, or the one who will finally give you the love you need.

You might tell yourself that you wouldn't fall for it, that you would keep yourself closed off—but are you really sure? If you haven't done the work needed for real healing, your own need to be loved can lead you astray, causing you to miss the signs and get fooled again.

Rather than isolating yourself to stay safe from narcissists, the safest course of action is to build healthy boundaries. If you interact with other people from a strong place, you'll be able to spot potential abusers before they spot you—thus allowing you to explore new relationships without unnecessary fear.

Here are seven tips to help you avoid toxic relationships in the future:

1. **Don't rush**: Don't be too quick to commit to new romantic relationships, friendships, or business partnerships. Take the time you need to get to know people before you let them in.
2. **Stay on guard**: Don't share information about your own vulnerabilities lightly. This means not telling the story of your past abuse history until you know the other person well.
3. **Don't make yourself responsible for other people**: Don't try to save people or become their caregiver. Let people be responsible for their own lives.
4. **Don't make other people responsible for you**: Don't look for someone to heal your wounds, to save you from loneliness, or to take charge of your life. Seek completion and wholeness inside yourself.

5. **Watch out for red flags**: Learn the symptoms of narcissism and the Dark Triad and watch out for them when you interact with other people.
6. **Be wary of your blind spots**: Be especially cautious when you are especially interested.
7. **Listen up**: Narcissists and other manipulators will give themselves away. Listen to what they're really saying and believe them when they expose who they really are.

Don't Rush

Not rushing into new relationships is the single most effective thing you can do to protect yourself from narcissistic abuse. When a narcissist goes looking for narcissistic supply, he doesn't want to waste his time or energy. Like a hungry predator, his best strategy is always to take the most vulnerable prey.

That's why narcissists so often push for a quick commitment or try to escalate the relationship as fast as possible. In a romantic relationship, this might mean saying "I love you" much quicker than people normally do or suggesting that you move in together, that you are soulmates, or that no one else understands you. In a new friendship, it might mean insisting that the two of you are "brothers" and that you are deeply loyal to each other even though in reality you hardly know each other. In a business situation, it might mean pushing for the two of you to go into business together without any real history or information.

In each of these cases, not rushing will protect you from the risk that the new person in your life is another narcissist. If he has sincere intentions (and perhaps just got carried away by his own enthusiasm), he'll respect your request to slow things down. When you don't agree to escalate the relationship before you're really ready, the narcissist will either move on to an easier target or show his hand by trying to blackmail you emotionally.

Any attempt to emotionally blackmail you is a dead giveaway, so if this happens, you can congratulate yourself on having smoked out a narcissist. Don't accuse them of anything or try to hold them accountable. Just quietly move on with your life in the knowledge that you successfully kept yourself safe from being harmed again.

Stay on Guard

In the sport of fencing, the "on guard" position is one in which the opponent cannot easily score a point against you because all your targets are covered. As a fencer in a tournament, you should never be too quick to uncover your target areas.

For example, most people are curious about the relationship history of whoever they're dating, but most people also know that it can be a bad idea to talk too much about past relationships in the first few dates. Usually, the reason for this is so that they don't seem obsessed with past partners or "the one that got away," but it can also help protect you against a narcissistic abuser.

If you talk about your past abuse history before you know a person very well, you could be giving a narcissist all the information they need to take advantage of you. By presenting himself as the exact opposite of whoever has hurt you in the past, a narcissist can slip past all your defenses and victimize you just as badly as the previous abuser.

Information about your vulnerabilities should be shared carefully, and only after establishing a basis for trust. Not seeing any obvious vulnerabilities, the frustrated narcissist will slip away to find an easier target.

If a new person in your life is too quick to reveal their own vulnerabilities or a history of unhappy relationships, you should consider this a warning sign. It isn't always an indication that the person is a narcissist, but it can still be a sign that they are codependent and not in a position to build a healthy relationship. In some cases, it can be a deliberate manipulative strategy. A narcissist will sometimes share highly personal information just to get you to do the same, beginning the process of escalating the relationship too quickly.

Don't Make Yourself Responsible for Other People

If you have a history of codependency, your instincts will always tell you to put other people's needs ahead of your own. Of course, most people are happy to take care of loved ones when they really need it. Codependency goes far beyond that healthy instinct, erasing the self to care for the other.

You may have had this tendency for a long time, quite possibly since early childhood. You probably did everything you could to take care of your abuser, perhaps in an attempt to heal his wounds or save him from his own worst tendencies. It didn't work, because he simply absorbed whatever you had to give and kept demanding more. The narcissist is a black hole that can never be filled.

As much as you might want to believe that you can heal someone with your love and care, it isn't really possible to do that for other people. The people who love us can give support us and be there for us, but we all have to heal our own wounds. Your instinct for self-sacrifice cannot help the narcissist, but it can do you tremendous harm.

Don't make yourself responsible for other people, and don't tell yourself that you can save or heal them. If someone you know is making self-destructive choices, don't shield them from the natural consequences. Don't make it your mission to fix another person's life.

The hardest thing for a codependent person is to know where the self ends and where the other begins. Teaching yourself healthy boundaries will keep you safe from narcissists and manipulators, and will it also make your other relationships happier and healthier. To establish clear boundaries, all you have to do is remember this simple phrase:

"I am not responsible for other people. I am only responsible for myself."

Don't Make Other People Responsible for You

This is the flip side of not making yourself responsible for other people. No one else can heal you; no one else can save you; no one else can complete you or make you whole. The idea that another person can do that for you is not just a romantic fantasy, but a description of codependent neediness. As long as you are looking for someone else to save or heal you, you will always be vulnerable to abusive narcissists.

This doesn't mean you can't love anyone. It doesn't mean that you can't fall in love. It just means that you can't think of love as a cure-all medicine, a way to get all your needs met or to erase the pain you may have experienced. Loving another person is about that person, not about what they can do for you.

Many therapists consider narcissism to be a type of codependency, and narcissists and codependents do have a number of things in common. One of those things is the tendency to idealize the concept of falling in love—in fact, fantasies about an ideal romance are one of the criteria for diagnosing narcissism. In the case of the narcissist, idealization is followed by devaluation. In the case of the codependent, idealization is followed by denial and disappointment.

Building healthy boundaries is essential for healing, and for keeping you safe from potential abusers. Give up on the idea of being saved by love and look to yourself to build a life that feels complete. When you do meet a new person, you'll be able to meet them as an equal—a much stronger basis for lasting love.

Watch Out for Red Flags

When you're getting to know a new person, watch out for red flags. Warning signs that something is wrong should not be ignored, because they almost always tell you something important about the person.

Not every potential abuser has full-blown Narcissistic Personality Disorder. Some people have other conditions, and some have narcissistic traits mixed with traits from other disorders. Many abusers fit a profile known as the "Dark Triad"—a mix of three different personality characteristics in varying amounts, including narcissism, psychopathy, and Machiavellianism.

Narcissistic traits include grandiosity, arrogance, entitlement, and self-centeredness.

Psychopathic traits include impulsive behavior, lack of empathy, and shallow emotional responses.

Machiavellian traits include being manipulative, calculated, and selfish.

A person with a Dark Triad personality is likely to become abusive or do you harm, even if she doesn't fit the diagnostic criteria for a specific disorder like Narcissistic Personality Disorder. To be diagnosed with NPD, you need to have five of the nine known traits of the disorder. A person might only have three or four of them, but in combination with a few traits of the Psychopathic personality and a tendency to be Machiavellian, that person can still be tremendously harmful.

The goal is not just to avoid narcissists, but to avoid toxic relationships altogether. Here are some of the red flags you'll need to watch out for:

- A self-centered attitude or a lack of genuine interest in other people
- Wanting always to be the center of attention
- Interrupting, talking over you, or not listening when you speak
- Treating you inconsiderately or disrespectfully
- Ignoring your boundaries
- Arrogance and superiority
- Excessive bragging
- Constant criticism and fault-finding
- Mistreatment of waiters, service people, and so on

- Manipulative behavior such as emotional blackmail, to you or others
- Controlling behavior
- An attitude of entitlement or demands for special treatment

Don't only pay attention to how this person treats you, but to how he treats the other people in his life. You can learn a lot about a person's character just by watching how they treat baristas and other service people, how they treat their family, and how they treat their exes. Be especially wary of anyone who only has negative things to say about past relationships. There's no reason to believe you will be the exception. In addition, extreme negativity about past relationships can indicate a self-serving and self-deceptive mindset.

Be Wary of Your Blind Spots

Anytime that you are especially interested in or attracted to a new person, you should be especially cautious. Why? For two main reasons. One, there's a risk that the type of person you're naturally drawn to is more likely to be narcissistic. We often repeat patterns in life without knowing exactly why, and a narcissist will often feel familiar and comfortable to a person whose most important relationships have been with narcissists. Two, we have a natural tendency to disregard the negative when we're focused on the positive. This can turn into denial very quickly and may lead you to ignore red flags and warning signs or to interpret them as being something else.

If you feel a strong physical attraction to a new person, you may minimize or even fail to notice the little signs that something is not quite right with this person. The excitement you feel when you're around them can blind you to things that would otherwise be obvious. If you're high on the positive feelings of a new romance, you might not want to ask yourself if you're love-bombed.

Being extra cautious doesn't mean being paranoid. You don't need to obsess over the what-ifs. Just take it slow, and time will reveal everything you need to know. If the new person is trying to manipulate you, they won't stick around when you insist on taking the time to get to know them properly. If they're sincere, they'll stick around long enough for you to feel comfortable.

Listen Up

Narcissists often give themselves away, and you can spot the warning signs if you pay attention. Sometimes, this is as straightforward as can be—if someone tells you they're "good at manipulation," believe them the first time.

Sometimes, it's more a matter of spotting patterns. There are exceptions, but generally speaking, the most accurate way to predict future behavior is to assume it will be the same as past behavior.

Does he admit to cheating in past relationships? Then he will cheat in this one. Does she admit to lying? Then she'll lie to you too. Does he describe himself as having a temper issue, a commitment issue, or a tendency to be jealous? He'll be the exact same way with you.

One of the biggest warning signs you should look out for is the "crazy ex" story. Everyone probably has one, but the narcissist will have a lot more than one. Remember: narcissists and other abusers do gaslight their victims, trying to make them believe they're crazy. If he keeps telling you all his exes were crazy, you can assume he will eventually be telling someone else how crazy you were.

At the very least, it shows either questionable judgment (why does he keep dating all these "crazy" people?) or a tendency to blame the other person for everything and take no responsibility. At worst, it can be a sign that he gaslights all his partners and that you will be next if you let it happen.

Conclusion

Thank you for making it through to the end of *Narcissistic Abuse: The Complete Guide to Healing*! Let's hope it was informative and able to provide you with all of the tools you need to achieve your goals—whatever they may be.

In this book, you've learned how to spot the signs and symptoms of narcissistic abuse and the common manipulative strategies and behaviors of the narcissist.

You've learned about narcissistic parenting and the roots of narcissism in childhood experiences.

You've learned how the narcissist really thinks, including the distinction between the ideal self and the true self, as well as narcissistic self-hatred.

You've learned why some people are more likely to be victimized by narcissistic abuse, as well as how codependency works.

You've learned effective tips and strategies for dealing with narcissists, including how to set boundaries and use assertive language.

You've learned what you can do if you have experienced narcissistic abuse, including how to take steps to improve your self-esteem, as well as how to get out of an abusive relationship.

You've learned the steps to healing from narcissistic abuse, as well as how to protect yourself in your future relationships by taking your time and maintaining healthy boundaries.

The next step is to put this information to good use. Whether you have a narcissist in your life or are in recovery from narcissistic abuse, this book can help you—but only if you *apply* it in your own relationships. This book may even be able to help you if you suspect have narcissistic traits yourself—and if it inspires you to seek the help, you need to learn more effective coping strategies.

Finally, if you found this book useful in any way, a review on Amazon is always appreciated!

Printed in Great Britain
by Amazon